HUTCHINSON ENGLISH TEXTS

W. H. AUDEN

A Selection

HUTCHINSON ENGLISH TEXTS

W. H. AUDEN

A Selection

With notes and a critical essay by

RICHARD HOGGART

HUTCHINSON EDUCATIONAL

HUTCHINSON EDUCATIONAL LTD
178–202 Great Portland Street, London W1

London Melbourne Sydney
Auckland Bombay Toronto
Johannesburg New York

First published April 1961
Reprinted February 1963
Reprinted January 1964
Reprinted July 1965
Reprinted August 1969

Printed in Great Britain by litho on smooth wove paper
by Anchor Press, and bound by Wm. Brendon,
both of Tiptree, Essex

09 062990 6

ACKNOWLEDGEMENTS

My thanks are due, first of all, to Mr Auden and Messrs Faber & Faber Ltd for permission to reprint the poems in this selection. I am also very grateful to my colleagues G. S. Fraser, P. H. Powell and E. Rushworth—and to my wife—for much help in preparing the edition.

Preface

The grouping of the poems within this selection has been decided by an unusual but, it is hoped, useful idea. This idea is explained in the first part of the Introduction. The remaining parts of the Introduction aim to give a critical foundation for understanding the nature, the range and variety, of Auden's work, and follow the group-by-group arrangement of the selection.

Within each section the poems are arranged in roughly chronological order, by volume-publication. The texts of the poems are the latest available. Auden is never tired of altering his poems, and it seems just to use the most recent version in each instance. Where the poems have titles, these too have been given by Auden, sometimes long after the poem was written.

The Notes are meant to give information and provoke thought. They name the sources of the poems and explain allusions which may puzzle. Unusual words are defined only if they are not likely to be found in most dictionaries. Sometimes the Notes make comments, invite comparisons, or refer to significant amendments by Auden. They are meant to suggest possible (not comprehensive or final) ways of approaching the poems, to prompt a fuller and more critical reading.

It may be worth adding that Auden has recorded some of these poems. His way of reading the later poems, in particular, is often enjoyable and helpful.

R.H.

Contents

Section Two: MAINLY THE THIRTIES

Section Three: LYRICS, SONGS AND
MUSICAL PIECES

Section Five: THEMES AND ARGUMENT

Introduction

I

The Shape and Nature of this Selection

W. H. Auden is alive today and still writing poetry. His latest book of poems, *About the House*, appeared in 1966. He will be sixty-two this year (1969) and has been publishing for almost forty years. Most of you who read this selection from his first thirty years as a writer are likely, therefore, to grow up and enter an adult society in which Auden's poetry is still appearing and being for the first time discussed. You may well see the appearance of several new volumes.

Why should such a poet, about much of whose work critical opinion has not yet settled, merit a volume chiefly intended for study by senior pupils in schools? There would be little problem if we were able to answer, quite firmly, that Auden is undoubtedly a poet of the first rank. Hardly anyone would make such a claim, though some of us have said—by now it seems for a very long time—that he may have the makings of such a poet. On the other hand, some say that though Auden is technically gifted and intellectually alert he consistently misuses each of these talents—is far too often technically showy, and intellectually merely fashionable. Whatever his final achievement, I believe this volume shows that, though few of his poems are faultless, he has produced a considerable amount of valuable—memorable, intelligent, witty and moving—verse. Further, few poets have so sharply illuminated some of the main social and individual problems of our time. By his attention to man-in-society and to the inner, spiritual, dilemmas which affect us all, Auden has helped to expose our period. He throws light, too, on the relation of the poet to language, to belief and to his audience (as in *Prospero to Ariel*). Auden's faults and contradictions are in themselves revealing if we wish seriously to study poetry and the poet's temptations, and particularly if we seek to understand better the pressures on poets in the middle twentieth century.

An attentive reading of Auden may therefore help us, first, to appreciate the work of an important living English poet. If it is a truly critical reading it may tell us something about the proper reading of any poet—living or dead—and about the poet's relationships with the world outside and with his own inner being.

.   .   .   .   .

The sections into which the poems have been grouped are not meant to put Auden's work into a hard mould, but to encourage a flexible reading of it. In the two available collections of his shorter poems, Auden himself has used different approaches. In the earlier *Collected Shorter Poems* (1950) he arranged the poems in alphabetical order of opening lines—which effectively discouraged any attempt to follow a trend or development. In his *Collected Shorter Poems 1927–57* (1966) he relented and printed the poems in chronological order of composition. This second approach seemed at first an obviously useful one here. But still it did not seem the *most* useful approach. Other possibilities then suggested themselves, such as dividing the poems according to their formal organization, or arranging them so as to show the pattern of Auden's thought as it alters over the three decades. Each of these seemed finally too rigid and the second, in particular, would invite us to read Auden for the meaning or 'message' and to forget that the meaning is part of the very texture of the poem, not a load carried on a decorated vehicle.

But as a result of reading and re-reading Auden's poems in order to choose those to be included here, a reasonably natural order or grouping did suggest itself. It seemed that, when one thought about Auden's work as a whole, one was aware of a pattern of overlapping interests and impressions (and the over-lapping is crucial). Thus, though one might first think of him as a social, a psychological or a religious poet, such a view did not suggest his characteristic tones, moods and settings—his particular temper. What is this temper? Throughout his verse a strange mixture, a compound of homely regard and lonely wandering, recurs. So much of his verse celebrates 'birth of a natural order and of love' in a relaxed, friendly and tender way ('Taller today, we remember similar evenings'; 'Out on the lawn I lie in bed'; 'Now from my window-sill I watch the night'). So much celebrates the landscape of home and neighbourhood. Yet at the same time so much is about wandering ('To throw away the key and walk away'), about harsh, isolated and lonely landscapes. Between these two poles we find the peculiarly Audenesque *personal* tones, distinct from the more 'objective' tones of that political or psychological or religious verse we may first recall. So it seemed right to begin with a group of poems which illustrate these characteristics.

After this, the shape began to emerge more easily. Auden's poetry of the Thirties, in so far as it especially shows social and psychological observation (his later poetry often has these qualities too, of course, though not so consistently), forms inevitably a section of its own. But many of its qualities are not to be explained solely by Auden's immediate interests at that time. They are part of the bent or stress of his mind—a mind which is fascinated by the *detail* of life and actions. So there are included in this section other examples—from later periods—of what I have called 'conversational verse', verse of acute comment.

Another obvious group, and a fruitful foil to the emphasis given by that above, was of Auden's songs and lyrics. It is easy to forget, as we note his quick intellectual activity, that all his life Auden has written lyrics. He so far broke the deliberate disorder in the *Collected Shorter Poems* as to give a separate section to what he called 'Songs and other musical pieces'.

The fourth group also is not meant primarily to illustrate Auden's themes or subjects. It contains poems which, taken together, illustrate the range and power of his technical skills outside the lyric. At this point the main emphasis falls on Auden's exercises in the sonnet (they are almost always allegorical sonnets), and on his comic or light-hearted verse.

In spite of all I have said against the tendency to view Auden in too narrowly intellectual a way, he is a poet who through his verse more often than not explores intellectual issues; which often turn out to be ultimately spiritual ones. Something of this is bound to have become evident in reading the section on his poetry of the Thirties. But there is a remarkable continuity in his thought, in his themes, in the arguments he has always carried on in his verse, a continuity which has been made especially plain since the war. So here emerged the fifth and final section, of poems showing the varied treatment of Auden's recurrent themes.

It follows, and is most important, that many of the poems could be placed in more than one of these sections. Sometimes Auden will write a lyric or sonnet about themes central to his thought; or a poem about home and wandering in the first section might just as well have been placed in two or three other sections. The groupings in this volume are meant to be provisional and suggestive. Read as constituents of these sections, the poems are being seen from only one angle; the sections as a whole suggest one series of ways of looking at Auden. But any valuable poem can be approached in several ways, and to be appreciated properly needs to be seen in as many ways as possible. If we shake up all these poems we will find that, as in a kaleidoscope, they will re-form into other groups. Each grouping could be justified, and would be interesting and revealing.

II

Early Life and Background; Characteristic Moods and Settings; the Landscapes of Home and of Wandering

(Section 1)

W. H. Auden was born at York, in 1907, into a professional middle-class family. His father was a Medical Officer of Health with wide interests. The family soon moved to Birmingham, where Auden gained first-hand experience of economic depression. He was given an education typical of his class and time. He went to a public school (Gresham's, Holt, Norfolk) and so to Oxford University in the middle Twenties. At school he talked first of being an engineer and read books on mining and geology (the contrast with the vocation of poet is not, in Auden's case, as striking as it might seem at first sight). In his later years at school Auden began to write poetry. Thomas Hardy was his first model, a good model since Hardy is a splendid and idiosyncratic versifier and a deeply humane writer. Hardy is also an uneven poet; as Auden has remarked, he does not discourage a young poet by showing consistent technical mastery. At his Oxford college, Christ Church, Auden wrote poetry continually and by then was claiming that T. S. Eliot was the only fit modern exemplar for a young poet. He began to acquire a reputation as a 'character'. He helped to edit *Oxford Poetry*, an annual collection. After leaving Oxford he spent some time in pre-Hitler Germany (the Germany of Christopher Isherwood's *Goodbye to Berlin*); the grim Thirties were just beginning. Once back in England, Auden was for a short time a schoolmaster and seems to have deeply enjoyed it. He has much of the teacher in his composition: he likes explaining things; he can be sympathetic without being sentimental, interested and affectionate towards people without being soft; he has a disciplinary streak.

He is deeply attached also to the English landscape. This might seem so common an attachment as not to be worth noticing. Yet sometimes we say we like the English scene without being clear just what we like, or perhaps have a stereotyped picture of thatched cottages and winding lanes. Auden knew quite early what kinds of landscape he likes and why. He likes, first, industrial landscapes, densely packed landscapes which are pockmarked with the evidence of intensive human endeavour and ingenuity—'the soiled productive cities' of the Black Country, the mining areas, the Lancashire cotton-belt (he once said that the view of Lancashire's mills from the top of the Pennines was one of the finest man-made sights in the world). 'Tramlines and slagheaps, pieces of machinery / That was, and is, my ideal scenery,' he wrote. All such landscapes bring home to him that man is a maker, a struggling but inventive creature using mind and hands and making a home wherever there is suitable space to settle. This interest dominates almost all Auden's geographical passages. He is only rarely interested in natural scenes for or in themselves; his geography is almost always human—economic or political—geography (as in *Macao* or *Spain*). What, he asks, does this landscape mean to men? What history have they stamped on it? In such passages his landscape is a backcloth to human activity.

Auden likes also bare and upland settings, especially mountainous regions wrested into stark and improbable shapes by glacial action. He loved walking with his father in the upper Pennines and during much of his time in New York, years later, his bedside book was a study of the mineralogy of the Lake District. He rarely refers to what might be called typical Sussex countryside or to that kind of landscape which—though it is not the only kind he describes—we often find in Tennyson, a rich and heavy landscape of hollyhocks and warm meadows (see *Dover, 1937*). If Auden's landscape is to be cluttered he prefers it to be cluttered with the evidence of man's industrial toil; if it is to be bare he prefers it bleakly bare. To this bare landscape he is drawn not only for itself but because, as he might well say, it speaks to him; it becomes symbolic for him in a way we must consider later. By instinct he thinks through images of land-scape; he speaks of 'villages of the heart', 'suburbs of fear' and 'our landscape of pain'—sometimes so easily that it seems almost automatic.

If we had space to suggest only one picture of Auden, and if this picture had to be as nearly as possible representative, we would show a landscape and a wanderer, a man on a Quest (as in the *Quest* sonnets). The figure of the Wanderer, the isolated man on a search, appears more frequently than any other in Auden's poetry. The Wanderer can take many forms. In the earliest verse he may be called the Airman or the Leader or the Hawk. He is physically isolated and surveys from a great height the interesting but muddled life of those below; he can see a possible order in the muddle which they do not see, and he would like to help it emerge. He is detached and slightly clinical. He is compassionate but also rather coldly reformative. Auden's is a strongly abstracting and generalizing intelligence; though he loves particular details, he wants always to relate them to a larger pattern. He does not naturally possess a loving sub-mission to particular things in themselves, to the varied 'this-ness' of life (the word is from G. M. Hopkins, who loved the 'thisness' of individual things); and he often too quickly *uses* his observation of individual human habits, rather than sits before them in humility.

Or the Wanderer may move across vast and empty land-scapes—plains, mountains, the spaces of the sea. It is entirely typical that Auden's first volume of prose criticism, *The En-chafèd Flood* (1951), should be about sea and desert imagery and symbolic wanderings across them; and one of the first operas for which he wrote the libretto was *The Rake's Progress*—in Auden's

version the Rake becomes, again, a Wanderer across the face of
the earth. But usually Auden's Wanderer is not so much
escaping challenges as positively seeking order.

So one might follow the Wanderer figure throughout
Auden's poetry, or one might follow the varying appearances
of his landscapes. One would constantly see the two as inter-
linked. A group of recent poems is called simply *Bucolics*, poems
about landscapes. Here the landscapes are of that second,
symbolic kind mentioned briefly above (what 'symbolic landscape' means here may be better understood from a reading of
the passage from *New Year Letter* in the first section of this selection). Auden, we have seen, has a mind which naturally makes
patterns and symbols. He discovered early that involved or
geometrically patterned landscapes, or the relations between
types of landscape (plains and mountains; valley and sea),
pulled at him with a strength which could not be adequately
explained by such a phrase as 'the attraction of natural beauty'.
They seemed to make visible to his imagination—without at
first being consciously formulated—the shapes of struggles
within the human will. They were symbols of human dilemmas,
though he had not deliberately tried to make them into symbols.

In some of these later landscape poems Auden has used a
long loping line which follows the movement of his thought as
he explores the peculiar symbolic hold the landscape has upon
him. We may see this by looking more closely at part of the poem
In Praise of Limestone, the whole of which is printed in Section 1:

If it form the one landscape that we the inconstant ones
Are consistently homesick for, this is chiefly
Because it dissolves in water. Mark these rounded slopes
With their surface fragrance of thyme and beneath
A secret system of caves and conduits; hear these springs
That spurt out everywhere . . . .
                   . . . . examine this region
Of short distances and definite places——

The long verse-sentence (the structure of the lines is described
in the Notes) has an easy spoken quality; it mixes colloquialism
and serious observation, wit and moral concern—though sometimes the tone relaxes into a deliberate facetiousness. The
poem's shape and its sinuous movement act out, as it were, the
meditation within the poet's mind. As he looks at these large
limestone hills above the wide plains and the fertile valleys, the
scene becomes both actually and symbolically moving to him;
it begins to stand for some of the complex struggles, the tensions, in human wills and motives—between man's urge to
settle and domesticate, and his urge to wander; between men as
quiet and gregarious beings and men as isolated or power-
seeking beings; between those who think they can tame life and
those who listen to deeper rhythms:

> Adjusted to the local needs of valleys
> Where everything can be touched or reached by walking,
> Their eyes have never looked into infinite space . . .
>   That is why, I suppose,
> The best and worst never stayed here long but sought
> Immoderate soils where the beauty was not so external,
> The light less public and the meaning of life
> Something more than a mad camp. 'Come!' cried the granite
>   wastes . . .

So the poem explores this landscape and these relationships
and closes on a view in perspective of the statues ('useless' to our
puritan or utilitarian minds, but not without meaning) that
man makes out of this same soft rock:

>   But if
> Sins can be forgiven, if bodies rise from the dead,
>   These modifications of matter into
> Innocent athletes and gesticulating fountains,
>   Made solely for pleasure, make a further point:

The blessed will not care what angle they are regarded from,
   Having nothing to hide. Dear, I know nothing of
Either, but when I try to imagine a faultless love
   Or the life to come, what I hear is the murmur
Of underground streams, what I see is a limestone landscape.

This is only one of the latest in a long line of Auden's landscapes, as we have seen—landscapes with many variations but
also with certain clearly defined dominant characteristics. Across
them the Wanderer moves, remembering his home fondly
but driven on by a desire to find order and meaning. There
is much in the figure that is plainly Auden himself, on a search
which now seems to occupy him more than the pursuit of
poetic excellence—the search for a life nearer to God's purposes.
But that search had begun a long time ago. It can be seen, if we
now use hindsight, in the very first poem in our selection ('From
the very first coming down'). And though the particular pre-
occupations of the Thirties may have obscured it, it was there
also throughout that time.

III

Auden in the Thirties; Social and Psychological Observation;
'Objective Reporting' and Conversational Verse

(Section 2)

Auden's first volume, *Poems*, appeared in 1930, at the opening of
a decade which is now beginning to acquire a slightly 'period'
flavour, especially for those not old enough to have known it.
What sort of a decade was it, to those who knew it as young
adults? It was, first, a peculiarly well-defined or boldly marked
period. 'A time of crisis and dismay' Auden called it, and no
other poet so captured the 'climate' of that time.

At home, unemployment grew sharply as the effects of the Wall Street Crash of 1929 spread into Europe. Unemployment hung massively over the decade until the effort of rearmament in its later years brought some dubious alleviation. This was the period of Depressed Areas and Means Tests, of 'The Threadbare Common Man / Begot on Hire-Purchase by Insurance'. It was, for far too many people—for the unemployed who marched from Jarrow in the North to state their case in London, for those who hung idle round street-corner lamp-posts, for the wives making do on little money about whom George Orwell wrote in *The Road to Wigan Pier*, for the shabby clerks and graduates who peddled gimcrack Japanese household goods from door to door—it was for all these a squalid and disheartened period.

Internationally, it was an even more menacing period, since it saw a giant's march to the world war of 1939–45. In Europe Mussolini had been the first of the major dictators to assume power; he was followed and soon surpassed by Hitler who became German Chancellor in 1933. The decade's crucial middle-point was the start of the Spanish Civil War in 1936, a dress rehearsal for 1939 (see *Spain, 1937*). Many who watched this sequence of events were horrified and alarmed at the rapid drift towards war. Yet many others, and of these some in the British Government, were inclined to minimize it and to talk of the effectiveness of 'appeasement'. These were the political members of what Auden called 'the old gang'.

In such a situation politics, domestic and international, were bound to loom large for intelligent and articulate young people. Auden belonged to a traditionally concerned group: that of the academically trained professional class intellectuals. He and those other poets who soon became known as The Auden Group (it was a community of ideas, not of mutually planned actions) were prepared to spend time on 'the flat ephemeral pamphlet and the boring meeting'. So this is also the period of the Popular Front meetings, of the Left Book Club and of Aid for Spain. There was, it is true, something rather too easily dramatic about much of this interest; it lent itself to a comfortably exciting 'goodies and baddies' feeling, a feeling that 'the old gang' were always hopelessly out of touch and wrong, and the new boys on the political Left always on the side of the angels. Yet the basic impulse was generous and charitable.

More important in any study of Auden, one has to be careful not to overestimate the extent, or misunderstand the nature, of his political commitment. He *was* politically interested and active; he did go to Spain for a short time during the Civil War; he did visit China to see the Sino-Japanese War at first-hand (see *Journey to a War*). Yet his political interest was always subordinate to his interest in the nature of man himself, in the roots of his social and individual problems; that is, in metaphysics. In the Thirties this interest often showed itself also as an attention to psychology (as in such poems as *Petition* and *A Free One*). He talked much of Freud and of many other psychologists; he interested himself particularly in loneliness, anxiety and fear, in 'the lost, the lonely, the unhappy'. We can now see that at bottom this concern was religious.

But there was, Auden and other writers felt, a specific and urgent job to be done in the Thirties. They had to look at their society and write about it as incisively as they could. Geoffrey Grigson, one of the most influential editors of the decade, exhorted them to be 'objective'; 'Report well. Begin with objects and events,' he urged. With this view Auden had much sympathy. He too exhorted his friends to be more 'clinical', to seek 'objective speech', to beware of romanticism and the excessively personal. We may well feel that such an attitude came more easily to Auden than to some of his friends (Stephen Spender, for instance). So much of Auden's verse at any time is in a sense detached, impersonal, briskly purposive. Some of his Thirties verse is spiritually muscular, a sort of moral gymnastics.

But the pressures of the day also helped to strengthen certain more valuable capacities in Auden. He has a naturally sharp eye for detail, for the revealing detail which indicates a habit of mind, a way of life, the nature of a social group:

> And nervous people who will never marry
> Live upon dividends in the old-world cottages
> With an animal for friend or a volume of memoirs.

It is acute, pithy, well observed. It is also a little too smart, too much like pinning and labelling a beetle. At its best, Auden's social and psychological observation of the Thirties produces—to use a phrase he would probably be happy to have applied to his poetry—'memorable speech'. When the poems work well they capture outlooks and settings in a way we do not easily forget. Auden cannot, however, usually sustain this kind of insight and control at length; we tend to remember isolated lines, couplets and stanzas (or a few short poems as a whole). They are the etched commentaries of an acute observer, or brief lyric meditations.

Much in the above comments might seem to have suggested that Auden is almost always tightly controlled and precise in expression. In parts he is; yet he is just as often large and rhetorical. He likes expressively dramatic flourishes ('The governess in the dead of night / Giving the universe nought for behaviour'—which is a melodramatic image and somewhat cruelly smart). Several of the weaknesses and most of the virtues of his predominant Thirties manner are to be found in the poem *Dover, 1937*, which may serve as an introduction to the poems in Section 2:

> Steep roads, a tunnel through the downs are the approaches:
> A ruined pharos overlooks a constructed bay;
> The sea-front is almost elegant; all this show
> Has, somewhere inland, a vague and dirty root:
>   Nothing is made in this town.

But the dominant Norman castle floodlit at night
And the trains that fume in the station built on the sea
Testify to the interests of its regular life:
Here live the experts on what the soldiers want
      And who the travellers are,

Whom the ships carry in and out between the lighthouses
That guard for ever the made privacy of this bay
Like twin stone dogs opposed on a gentleman's gate:
Within these breakwaters English is spoken; without
      Is the immense improbable atlas.

The eyes of the departing migrants are fixed on the sea,
To conjure their special fates from the impersonal water:
'I see an important decision made on a lake,
An illness, a beard, Arabia found in a bed,
      Nanny defeated, Money.'

And filled with the tears of the beaten or calm with fame,
The eyes of the returning thank the historical cliffs:
'The heart has at last ceased to lie, and the clock to accuse;
In the shadow under the yew, at the children's party
      Everything will be explained.'

And the old town with its keep and its Georgian houses
Has built its routine upon these unusual moments;
The vows, the tears, the slight emotional signals
Are here eternal and unremarkable gestures
      Like ploughing or soldiers' songs:

Soldiers who swarm in the pubs in their pretty clothes,
As fresh and silly as girls from a high-class academy:
The Lion, the Rose or the Crown will not ask them to die,
Not here, not now. All they are killing is time,
      Their pauper civilian future.

Above them, expensive and lovely as a rich child's toy,
The aeroplanes fly in the new European air,
On the edge of that air that makes England of minor
    importance;
And the tides warn bronzing bathers of a cooling star,
        With half its history done.

High over France the full moon, cold and exciting
Like one of those dangerous flatterers one meets and loves
When one is very unhappy, returns the human stare:
The night has many recruits; for thousands of pilgrims
        The Mecca is coldness of heart.

And the cry of the gulls at dawn is sad like work:
The soldier guards the traveller who pays for the soldier;
Each one prays in the dusk for himself and neither
Controls the years. Some are temporary heroes:
        Some of these people are happy.

      (*Another Time*, xxvii; Collected Shorter Poems, p. 121)

Dover, 1937 is about social and human relations. For Auden
the town has unusual interest and significance. As one of our
most famous harbours, our representative link with the world
outside this island, it sees both endings and beginnings. It is the
last point within the territory of 'the old gang', and in the
Thirties is seen as echoing their seediness, their hollow pre-
tensions and class snobberies. It is also a place from which
migrants depart—both those who are trying to run away from
themselves (from their psychological problems) and those
who seek positively to make a better life; or to which, frus-
trated or successful, migrants return.

From such a vantage point Auden is able to comment on the
condition of Europe and on England's relation to it; on the
character of 'frontier towns' and on the psychology of migrants
(again we meet the Wanderer theme). He can make subsidiary

allusions to the human geography of England (Dover is in the South and not industrial; it is, he seems to accuse, parasitic); and to England's social patterns (the soldiery, for instance). He can talk, as so often, about the 'lonelies', the frightened souls behind many of our bold personal façades, the sea of individual unhappiness and misery ('Each one prays in the dusk for himself').

Dover, 1937 is able to handle so much matter in so small a space because of the discipline in 'objective' writing described above. It can outline detail sharply, pick out the illuminating from the insignificant fact—the soldiers' public-house manners, the architecture of a place which combines seaside-resort-middle-class-country-town-military-centre-and-port. Once the reader is accustomed to the pithy item-by-item strokes of detail and comment and to the concentration of the epithets there are few obscurities. It is a pity that two of the last three stanzas are rather grandly slack; here the addiction to large gesture has led to inflation. But the poem recovers in its last verse and ends, as it has been for most of its length, suggestive, rooted in its place and period, epigrammatic and stimulating verse.

The tone is markedly easy and conversational. We are listening to the poet thinking aloud. In the volume of verse which Auden published at the end of this decade (*Another Time*) this conversational manner was predominant. Here Auden owes much to the example of W. B. Yeats, whose conversational verse he has always greatly admired. He has not been able to acquire Yeats's superb facility in this manner (see, for example, Yeats's *Easter, 1916*), but his achievement is not negligible. A short poem, *Musée des Beaux Arts*, might serve well to show the main virtues and weaknesses of this manner as Auden adopts it (the poem is in Section 2). With a laconic casualness it makes a searching and moving observation on human suffering, and this is its strength; it is also in parts both knowing and uneasily colloquial.

Even today Auden sometimes writes in a development of

28

this manner, in a relaxed low-temperature verse. This is often what he describes himself as 'unofficial poetry'. He has always insisted that poetry does not need to be consistently on its high horse; he has always liked to debunk the grand, the 'proper', the decorous and the official.

.   .   .   .

So the Thirties dragged to their grim but honourable con- clusion. Like many others—not writers alone—Auden had tried to fight against the trend towards war. It was hard, when war finally broke out, to decide whether their efforts had been rightly directed. Auden had gone on a visit to the United States at the end of 1938 and had remained there. When Germany finally launched her attack on Poland he surveyed from New York the first decade his generation had known as adults. This poem, *1st September, 1939* (written in the metre of Yeats's *Easter, 1916*), sums up the lessons of the experience as he understands them. Its conclusion is religious and so points to the new em- phases which were now more and more appearing in Auden's writing. It is obviously the most fitting epilogue to the Thirties as these poets, of whom Auden was the acknowledged leader, had known them.

IV

Lyrics and Songs; Sonnets and Other Forms; Comic Verse

(Sections 3 and 4)

Auden's technical skill, his poetic virtuosity, is indisputable; he is gifted, professional, a constant practiser. He has more than once said that he is interested in all forms of verse, from the word-of-mouth limerick to the closely designed poem of volume length. He has also said that he opposes all notions of artistic decorum and of 'correct' style. So we should expect great range and flexibility in his verse; and we find it. We find also a disposition to play around, just for the fun of it. This occasionally mars the poetry, but not always. It is important not to assume that 'playing around' in itself and automatically makes a poem faulty (as though 'high seriousness' were indispensable). Auden thinks that the primary characteristic of a budding poet is the wish to 'hang around words' and play with them—rather than the wish to reform the world or to become famous. Other professions may give such opportunities; only poetry starts by putting words into odd shapes.

As we move through Auden's poetry we notice a recurrent loyalty to a few forms, as well as a recurrent readiness to experiment. Two forms have obviously attracted him steadily: the brief lyric and the sonnet; we must look further at them later. In his first volume he wrote some curt and gnomic poems which obviously owed something to the poetry of Laura Riding and Robert Graves (*This Lunar Beauty*; *This One* are two of these). We have discussed the epigrammatic and conversational verse which followed; and in that same period Auden intermittently wrote ballads, songs with choruses and some poems in little-used forms such as the villanelle, the sestina and the canzone (see especially Section 4). His comic verse has been fed from several sources: army songs, music-hall and cabaret, jazz. He has from time to time, but notably in *The Age of Anxiety*, modified the alliterative line of Anglo-Saxon poetry; a brief explanation of this line will be found in the Notes. He has been interested in, and has written interestingly about, the challenge presented by opera libretti—the difficulty of writing a clearly running line which can be sung without confusing the singer or the hearer with a complicated interplay of suggestion, and which is yet not simply banal.

These are only typical instances from a wide range of activity by a mind deeply interested in *craft*, in the formal-play element in poetry. In suitable conditions, Auden might well have enjoyed being a court-poet. He would probably have been the court-wit at the same time, but a dry and telling wit—for his 'play' usually does have, indirectly, a moral purpose.

When we think of the characteristic texture of Auden's verse we are reminded first of those impersonal and external qualities which were noted earlier. His poems are not strong in some sensory effects. He has a fine ear (as poems such as *Seascape* and *Lullaby* amply show); he responds well to patterns of colour —but seems more interested in the patterns than in the modulations of the colours themselves. There is little touch, taste or smell in his verse. He rarely lingers over his sensory effects— except when they are aural—and seems not greatly interested in them for themselves. We tend to remember his poems as shapes, as patterns of observation and analysis. He once said that he tends to see his own poems as 'squares and oblongs'; that is, presumably, as structures formed out of the interplay of man's moral dilemmas. The emphasis is once again on pattern.

Similarly, his epithets do not usually carry rich sensory evocations. Lines such as these, from *Macbeth*:

> Light *thickens*; and the crow
> Makes wing to the *rooky* wood:

would hardly be likely to occur in Auden's poetry. At their most characteristic his epithets do not physically describe the objects they qualify; they are, rather, conceptual. They comment rather than describe; they set the object into a relationship with something or someone else. Often they appear in pairs so that the two adjectives set off an intellectual friction. Auden is likely to say, not 'grassy slope', but 'tolerant enchanted slope'. He does not write:

> Lay your graceful head, my love,
> Golden on my circling arm

31

but

> Lay your sleeping head, my love,
> Human on my faithless arm

and the interest comes from the play of moral relations between the owners of the head and arm.

Not much need be said about Auden's favourite and recurrent technical habits; nearly all of them are clever but some clever-clever. During the Thirties in particular he made use of a type of simile in which a concrete fact was yoked to an abstract idea. This might produce an effective surprise or might seem merely smart:

> Problems like relatives standing

> Will Ferdinand be as fond of a Miranda
> Familiar as a stocking.

He has always been fond of dying falls, especially dying falls with three steps:

> That wept, and grew enormous, and cried Woe.

He has often used a sort of stylized 'pointing', by means of successive definite articles:

> The boarding-house food, the boarding-house faces,
> The rain-spoilt picnics in the windswept places,
> The camera lost and the suspicion,

But many of these habits have fallen away during the last few years; today his most frequent excess is in adopting highly unusual words, dictionary-raiding and word-coining.

.   .   .   .   .

Auden's lyrics, as we have said, form by now a substantial

group within his work and one which can claim considerable
admiration. They have some striking common qualities. Most
of them create a sense of stillness, the stillness of harmony and
calm, or the stillness of menace. They reflect and muse. This is
strange, in view of the quick and rather jackdaw-like activity
of so much of Auden's poetry. Then one remembers that he
quotes more than once—as though it were a reminder and
corrective to his own immediate tendencies—Rilke's insistence
on the need for a poet to sit still and absorb, to 'bless what there
is for being'.

May with its light behaving is a typical Audenesque lyric:

> May with its light behaving
> Stirs vessel, eye and limb;
> The singular and sad
> Are willing to recover,
> And to the swan-delighting river
> The careless picnics come,
> The living white and red.
>
> The dead remote and hooded
> In their enclosures rest; but we
> From the vague woods have broken,
> Forests where children meet
> And the white angel-vampires flit;
> We stand with shaded eye,
> The dangerous apple taken.
>
> The real world lies before us,
> Animal motions of the young,
> The common wish for death,
> The pleasured and the haunted;
> The dying master sinks tormented
> In the admirers' ring;
> The unjust walk the earth.

And love that makes impatient
The tortoise and the roe, and lays
The blonde beside the dark,
Urges upon our blood,
Before the evil and the good
How insufficient is
The endearment and the look.

(Look, Stranger, xvi; *Collected Shorter Poems*, p. 244)

In spite of the stillness Auden is not, we soon realize, simply absorbing the scene; he is quickly into moral debate again. The allegro opening recalls the pleasure of a May morning, which urges even those held in the grip of their own neuroses to relax, to be happy simply in *being*. This is a moment of simple happiness and gentleness (evoked in part by the interplay of long and short 'i' sounds and by the quietly echoing pattern of predominantly off-rhymes or near-rhymes).

Thereafter the poem is sad. We respond to May much as the animals do, at first. But we also stand in the hard light of self-consciousness; we know the doubt of the double-personality, which acts and questions its actions. 'Love' prompts us as it prompts 'the tortoise and the roe'; but to our self-aware condition 'Love' soon shows itself as inadequate. Auden is already moving towards the more complex view of 'Love' which he examines in so much of his later work.

The third stanza, with its scraps of psychology, seems far too bitty and overloaded with items; it might have been omitted without much loss. And isn't 'vague' in the second stanza (Auden likes the word) so vaguely used as to become an invitation to the reader to supply what suggestions he pleases? By contrast there is an economical charge of meaning in:

The singular and sad
Are willing to recover,

and a fine conciseness in:

> To the swan-delighting river
> The careless picnics come

and in:

> We stand with *shaded* eye
> The dangerous apple taken.

.   .   .   .   .

Auden's sonnets are almost always compressed visual or dramatic stories, allegories of some moral problem, tightly held within the fourteen lines and the firm rhyme-scheme. Here again, Rilke is the ancestor. From him Auden learned much about the use of landscape as a symbol for abstract problems otherwise exceptionally difficult to express. 'One of the constant problems of the poet,' said Auden in a discussion of Rilke, 'is how to express abstract ideas in concrete terms.' Auden's sonnets often have in common with Rilke's an un-announced jump into the narrative, which forces the reader to pick up the legend as he goes along; a similar air of control; a similar unhurried assurance which comes partly from having firm symbols to manipulate.

Sometimes Auden seems to have become so skilled in this form that he gives the air of producing the sonnets by habit. At such times they have too glossy a finish; he over-works certain movements and phrasings and suggests that his theme has been too easily buttoned-up. Yet at their best the sonnets are good examples of memorable speech. This one shows some of the tricks, but is largely successful:

> So from the years the gifts were showered; each
> Ran off with his at once into his life:
> Bee took the politics that make a hive,
> Fish swam as fish, peach settled into peach.

And were successful at the first endeavour;
The hour of birth their only time at college,
They were content with their precocious knowledge,
And knew their station and were good for ever.

Till finally there came a childish creature
On whom the years could model any feature,
And fake with ease a leopard or a dove;

Who by the lightest wind was changed and shaken,
And looked for truth and was continually mistaken,
And envied his few friends and chose his love.

(In Time of War: i, *Collected Shorter Poems*, p. 271)

The theme—not in itself unusual—is one which, as we shall
see, occurs again and again in Auden. Man is a creature who is
forever *becoming*, hardly ever in a state of *being*; he is a double
creature, driven by will (free-will *and* wilfulness). The animal
and vegetable world (in the octave) simply *is*; without self-
consciousness, these things are what they are. Man has freedom
to choose, self-consciousness. The poem muses sadly over the
weight of consciousness on man but also celebrates it; for man
can love, can choose to love and choose when to love. He is
bound (bound to choose, even if he chooses not to choose) and
free (the way his choice falls depends on him). Hence the close
is far more positive than regretful.

V

Ideas and Argument; Themes and Development

(Section 5)

We have already noted that Auden went to America in 1938.
He stayed there and some years later became an American

citizen. His home is in New York, but he has spent much time travelling around America, sometimes teaching for a period at various universities. During the last few years he has kept a small summer home in Europe (first on the Italian island of Ischia and latterly in Austria), in which he may write quietly, away from the stuffy New York summer. In 1956 he was elected Professor of Poetry at the University of Oxford. This post is held for five years, and Auden therefore retired in 1961. During his tenure he spent each summer term (from after Easter to the end of June) in Oxford.

Some critics have said that by breaking his English connections Auden has severed roots essential to the success of his poetry. One can see grounds for such a view: in many of his likes and dislikes, in the peculiar fabric of his feelings (a dry gentleness, a complicated cranky independence, for instance), Auden is recognizably an English writer. Yet the main lines of his thought—and one cannot altogether separate his thought from his own sense of the poetic vocation and so from his poetry—draw upon themes common to all advanced Western societies. In this sense Auden is an unrooted poet, who might equally be at home in any one of the great representative centres of mid-twentieth-century Western life—in Manchester, London, Chicago, Berlin. One may even argue that, given the peculiar temper of his mind, New York—that vast metropolitan mass of 'willing' individuals—is his best home, the very symbol of much that lies at the heart of his poetry.

At that heart is a religious view of life, but one almost never withdrawn or mystical. He is, we now know, fascinated by man living on this earth, within societies he has made, fallible but struggling, moving along the tape of time but under the shadow of the timeless reality of God. We have noted that this was potentially true even in the Thirties, below the immediate political and psychological elements. Auden was never an orthodox Marxist or Freudian. There was always something more. We can follow the way in which this 'something more' commands increasing attention by watching his uses of one word, 'Love', throughout his poetry. He is often quixotic, but in this shows a remarkably steady development. At the beginning 'Love' had a rather undefined and vague meaning ('O Love, the interest itself in thoughtless Heaven'). It yet indicated a quality, both inside man and outside him, which went beyond what either Marxists or Freudians would have recognized. It was disciplined and social, not a self-love; but it was not Christian love. As Auden's thought developed, so this word took on fuller meanings, and eventually he meant by it Christian love, charity, Grace (see *The Prophets*). By then Auden had, of course, become a professed Christian. Of this argument within himself the fullest statement—an argument in couplets—is *New Year Letter*, the book-length poem which appeared in 1941.

Auden has always drawn sustenance from a few selected thinkers, though the thinkers change from time to time. Since the Forties, two of the most influential have been the Danish 'existentialist' theologian Søren Kierkegaard (1813–1855) and the living American theologian Reinhold Niebuhr. In Kierkegaard, to take only one instance, he was particularly interested to consider 'original anxiety', the basic insecurity of man which reflects his fallen nature and his possible salvation. Much in Niebuhr's thought bears on Auden's interest, not in the mystical, but in the moral dilemmas and social involvements of man living in time and space, held in the fruitful grip of choice, of freedom-with-necessity. These, and many other related themes, occur again and again in Auden's more recent verse. One example, earlier than most but typical, may throw light on the others printed here. This poem is called *Our Bias*:

> The hour-glass whispers to the lion's roar,
> The clock-towers tell the gardens day and night,
> How many errors Time has patience for,
> How wrong they are in being always right.

Yet Time, however loud its chimes or deep,
However fast its falling torrent flows,
Has never put one lion off his leap
Nor shaken the assurance of a rose.

For they, it seems, care only for success:
While we choose words according to their sound
And judge a problem by its awkwardness;

And Time with us was always popular.
When have we not preferred some going round
To going straight to where we are?
(*Another Time*, xv, Penguin Selection, p. 79)

It uses a contrast we have met before. Auden likes to muse over and draw morals from such contrasts. The animals and plants are in a state of simply *being* ('Simply they are,' he says elsewhere); man is never perfect or perfectly happy. Presumably no lion has ever looked up and asked itself, 'Am I a *good* lion?', let alone, 'Am I a *morally* good lion?' Man does this constantly, and Auden reflects on and celebrates the crucial fact—again, in that quiet, almost wry, tone we have noted before. It is compounded of sympathy for man's endless worried muddle, and pride at his energy and his urge to muddle through to something better. We are illogical and messy; for instance, we fall in love with words for their own sakes and refuse to use them simply as conventional signs. If we went straight to our objectives in life, we would not worry about whether the expedient course, the obviously effective course, was also the right course. We would simply follow it. Yet this disposition in itself can hold us back from finding the Truth in God. We can begin to enjoy the Quest, the going round and round, for its own sake. It defers the day of decision, of recognition of our humble and homely duty under God. We are wilful, worrying, maddening—but we choose; and Auden would be one of the last to regret it. He

remains humane and purposive; 'accept the present in its ful-
ness', he says; work towards building the Just City, even though
you know it can never be finally completed.

.　　　　.　　　　.　　　　.　　　　.

Until a few years ago, in spite of Auden's efficient profes-
sionalism, one was particularly conscious of certain irresolu-
tions in his verse. The four long poems which he wrote soon
after settling in America (*New Year Letter*, *The Sea and the Mirror*,
For the Time Being and *The Age of Anxiety*) show much of this
difficulty, as do many of the shorter poems written in the years
after. He was, for example, often unsure in his tone, affectedly
colloquial, showy or overbright; so that one wondered whether
his move to America—whatever its grounds—had cut him off
from that assurance of a known audience which he would
have had if he had remained in Britain.

There were deeper tensions, tensions between Auden the
man and Auden the believer, tensions between the believer and
the writer. Much of this can be seen in *Prospero to Ariel* (Section 5)
and in the long prose speech by Caliban in *The Sea and the Mirror*.
'Art is not enough,' says Auden more than once. Art—poetry—
is interesting and perhaps important; but in what sense is it
finally meaningful to the individual soul before God—not only
to the individual reader but to the individual creator, the poet
himself? It 'makes nothing happen'. His most typical single
phrase from many on this subject is that poetry is 'a game of
knowledge'. It is, first, a game—a form of magic and fun, a release, a playing around; it has fixed rules and needs discipline,
but something always depends on luck in the end. Yet it is also
in a certain sense concerned with knowledge, and its magic is
meaningful. The knowledge is, though, a by-product of the
play and comes indirectly, as in the serious absorbed play of a
child. In art's harmony and ritual are mirrored the possibility
of a greater order outside man's powers. So poetry can help to
'direct us to ourselves', can persuade us to a form of 'moral

rejoicing', can point to 'love and truth'. At this stage, we realize, we meet the fullest expression of Auden's urge to irradiate human activity with eternal meaning.

The debate is a long and subtle one and not yet completed; it will perhaps never be completed. Auden's latest volume (*About the House*) suggests that for the moment he is more strongly than ever inclined to think of poetry as 'verbal playing', that he is thinking less about what poetry can 'do', can reform. He still occasionally writes poems rooted in society (though always seen in relation to God—as in *Friday's Child*). But he often writes poems of quiet religious celebration (*Whitsunday in Kirchstetten*); or relaxed, playful, elaborate poems.

.   .   .   .   .

Auden does not seem likely ever to renounce the writing of poetry altogether, but it may well become increasingly marginal to him. Or he may discover new springs of interest in the writing of poetry. He has at the moment a supple and inscrutable ease in much of his work—like someone amusing himself cleverly on the piano.

Meanwhile, as we look back over the forty years of his work, we can attempt an interim estimate. He has produced a body of verse which commands our respect and admiration in a number of ways; he has been the brilliant and sometimes profoundly evocative explorer of dilemmas within the human will; in his vividly epigrammatic, conversational and alert verse he held a mirror to a complex decade; he has written a number of lyrics not likely to be soon forgotten. He has been deeply engaged in his time, and has produced some poetry which demands be judged outside the limitations of that time. He has set an example of devotion to art which few today can equal.

Characteristic Moods
and Settings

The Letter

From the very first coming down
Into a new valley with a frown
Because of the sun and a lost-way,
You certainly remain: to-day
I, crouching behind a sheep-pen, heard
Travel across a sudden bird,
Cry out against the storm, and found
The year's arc a completed round
And love's worn circuit re-begun,
Endless with no dissenting turn.
Shall see, shall pass, as we have seen
The swallow on the tile, spring's green
Preliminary shiver, passed
A solitary truck, the last
Of shunting in the Autumn. But now,
To interrupt the homely brow,
Thought warmed to evening through and through,
Your letter comes, speaking as you,
Speaking of much but not to come.

Nor speech is close nor fingers numb
If love not seldom has received
An unjust answer, was deceived.
I, decent with the seasons, move,
Different or with a different love,

Nor question overmuch the nod,
The stone smile of this country god
That never was more reticent,
Always afraid to say more than it meant.

The Watershed

Who stands, the crux left of the watershed,
On the wet road between the chafing grass
Below him sees dismantled washing-floors,
Snatches of tramline running to the wood,
An industry already comatose,
Yet sparsely living. A ramshackle engine
At Cashwell raises water; for ten years
It lay in flooded workings until this,
Its latter office, grudgingly performed,
And further here and there, though many dead
Lie under the poor soil, some acts are chosen
Taken from recent winters; two there were
Cleaned out a damaged shaft by hand, clutching
The winch the gale would tear them from; one died
During a storm, the fells impassable,
Not at his village, but in wooden shape
Through long abandoned levels nosed his way
And in his final valley went to ground.

Go home, now, stranger, proud of your young stock,
Stranger, turn back again, frustrate and vexed:
This land, cut off, will not communicate,
Be no accessory content to one
Aimless for faces rather there than here.
Beams from your car may cross a bedroom wall,
They wake no sleeper; you may hear the wind
Arriving driven from the ignorant sea

To hurt itself on pane, on bark of elm
Where sap unbaffled rises, being spring;
But seldom this. Near you, taller than grass,
Ears poise before decision, scenting danger.

Missing

From scars where kestrels hover,
The leader looking over
Into the happy valley,
Orchard and curving river,
May turn away to see
The slow fastidious line
That disciplines the fell,
Hear curlew's creaking call
From angles unforeseen,
The drumming of a snipe
Surprise where driven sleet
Had scalded to the bone
And streams are acrid yet
To an unaccustomed lip;
The tall unwounded leader
Of doomed companions, all
Whose voices in the rock
Are now perpetual,
Fighters for no one's sake,
Who died beyond the border.

Heroes are buried who
Did not believe in death
And bravery is now
Not in the dying breath
But resisting the temptations

To skyline operations.
Yet glory is not new;
The summer visitors
Still come from far and wide,
Choosing their spots to view
The prize competitors,
Each thinking that he will
Find heroes in the wood,
Far from the capital

Where lights and wine are set
For supper by the lake,
But leaders must migrate:
'Leave for Cape Wrath to-night,'
And the host after waiting
Must quench the lamps and pass
Alive into the house.

Taller To-day

Taller to-day, we remember similar evenings,
Walking together in a windless orchard
Where the brook runs over the gravel, far from the glacier.

Nights come bringing the snow, and the dead howl
Under headlands in their windy dwelling
Because the Adversary put too easy questions
On lonely roads.

But happy now, though no nearer each other,
We see farms lighted all along the valley;
Down at the mill-shed hammering stops
And men go home.

Noises at dawn will bring
Freedom for some, but not this peace
No bird can contradict: passing, but is sufficient now
For something fulfilled this hour, loved or endured.

The Journey

To throw away the key and walk away,
Not abrupt exile, the neighbours asking why,
But following a line with left and right,
An altered gradient at another rate,
Learns more than maps upon the whitewashed wall,
The hand put up to ask; and makes us well
Without confession of the ill. All pasts
Are single old past now, although some posts
Are forwarded, held looking on a new view;
The future shall fulfil a surer vow.
Not smiling at queen over the glass rim
Nor making gunpowder in the top room,
Not swooping at the surface still like gulls
But with prolonged drowning shall develop gills.
But there are still to tempt; areas not seen
Because of blizzards or an erring sign
Whose guessed at wonders would be worth alleging,
And lies about the cost of a night's lodging;
Travellers may sleep at inns but not attach;
They sleep one night together, not asked to touch,
Receive no normal welcome, not the pressed lip,
Children to lift, not the assuaging lap,
Crossing the pass descend the growing stream
Too tired to hear except the pulses' strum,
Reach villages to ask for a bed in,
Rock shutting out the sky, the old life done.

Chorus

Doom is dark and deeper than any sea-dingle.
Upon what man it fall
In spring, day-wishing flowers appearing,
Avalanche sliding, white snow from rock-face,
That he should leave his house,
No cloud-soft hand can hold him, restraint by women;
But ever that man goes
Through place-keepers, through forest trees,
A stranger to strangers over undried sea,
Houses for fishes, suffocating water,
Or lonely on fell as chat,
By pot-holed becks
A bird stone-haunting, an unquiet bird.

There head falls forward, fatigued at evening,
And dreams of home,
Waving from window, spread of welcome,
Kissing of wife under single sheet;
But waking sees
Bird-flocks nameless to him, through doorway voices
Of new men making another love.

Save him from hostile capture,
From sudden tiger's spring at corner;
Protect his house,
His anxious house where days are counted
From thunderbolt protect,
From gradual ruin spreading like a stain;
Converting number from vague to certain,
Bring joy, bring day of his returning,
Lucky with day approaching, with leaning dawn.

A Summer Night 1933

(To Geoffrey Hoyland)

Out on the lawn I lie in bed,
Vega conspicuous overhead
  In the windless nights of June,
As congregated leaves complete
Their day's activity; my feet
  Point to the rising moon.

Lucky, this point in time and space
Is chosen as my working-place,
  Where the sexy airs of summer,
The bathing hours and the bare arms,
The leisured drives through a land of farms
  Are good to the newcomer.

Equal with colleagues in a ring
I sit on each calm evening
  Enchanted as the flowers
The opening light draws out of hiding
With all its gradual dove-like pleading,
  Its logic and its powers

That later we, though parted then,
May still recall these evenings when
  Fear gave his watch no look;
The lion griefs loped from the shade
And on our knees their muzzles laid,
  And Death put down his book

Now north and south and east and west
Those I love lie down to rest;
  The moon looks on them all,

The healers and the brilliant talkers
The eccentrics and the silent walkers,
  The dumpy and the tall.

She climbs the European sky,
Churches and power-station lie
  Alike among earth's fixtures:
Into the galleries she peers
And blankly as a butcher stares
  Upon the marvellous pictures

To gravity attentive, she
Can notice nothing here, though we
  Whom hunger does not move,
From gardens where we feel secure
Look up and with a sigh endure
  The tyrannies of love:

And, gentle, do not care to know,
Where Poland draws her eastern bow,
  What violence is done,
Nor ask what doubtful act allows
Our freedom in this English house,
  Our picnics in the sun.

Soon, soon, through dykes of our content
The crumpling flood will force a rent
  And, taller than a tree,
Hold sudden death before our eyes
Whose river dreams long hid the size
  And vigours of the sea.

But when the waters make retreat
And through the black mud first the wheat
  In shy green stalks appears,

When stranded monsters gasping lie,
And sounds of riveting terrify
  Their whorled unsubtle ears,

May these delights we dread to lose,
This privacy, need no excuse
  But to that strength belong,
As through a child's rash happy cries
The drowned parental voices rise
  In unlamenting song.

After discharges of alarm
All unpredicted let them calm
  The pulse of nervous nations,
Forgive the murderer in his glass,
Tough in their patience to surpass
  The tigress her swift motions.

Paysage Moralisé

Hearing of harvests rotting in the valleys
Seeing at end of street the barren mountains,
Round corners coming suddenly on water,
Knowing them shipwrecked who were launched for islands,
We honour founders of these starving cities
Whose honour is the image of our sorrow,

Which cannot see its likeness in their sorrow
That brought them desperate to the brink of valleys;
Dreaming of evening walks through learned cities
They reined their violent horses on the mountains,
Those fields like ships to castaways on islands,
Visions of green to them who craved for water.

They built by rivers and at night the water
Running past windows comforted their sorrow;
Each in his little bed conceived of islands
Where every day was dancing in the valleys
And all the green trees blossomed on the mountains
Where love was innocent, being far from cities.

But dawn came back and they were still in cities;
No marvellous creature rose up from the water;
There was still gold and silver in the mountains
But hunger was a more immediate sorrow,
Although to moping villagers in valleys
Some waving pilgrims were describing islands . . .

'The gods,' they promised, 'visit us from islands,
Are stalking, head-up, lovely, through our cities;
Now is the time to leave your wretched valleys
And sail with them across the lime-green water,
Sitting at their white sides, forget your sorrow,
The shadow cast across your lives by mountains.'

So many, doubtful, perished in the mountains,
Climbing up crags to get a view of islands,
So many, fearful, took with them their sorrow
Which stayed them when they reached unhappy cities,
So many, careless, dived and drowned in water,
So many, wretched, would not leave their valleys.

It is our sorrow. Shall it melt? Ah, water
Would gush, flush, green these mountains and these valleys,
And we rebuild our cities, not dream of islands.

Through the Looking Glass

The earth turns over; our side feels the cold;
And life sinks choking in the wells of trees:

The ticking heart comes to a standstill, killed;
The icing on the pond waits for the boys.
Among the holly and the gifts I move,
The carols on the piano, the glowing hearth,
All our traditional sympathy with birth,
Put by your challenge to the shifts of Love.

Your portrait hangs before me on the wall,
And there what view I wish for I shall find,
The wooded or the stony, though not all
The painter's gifts can make its flatness round;
Though each blue iris see the heaven of failures,
That mirror world where Logic is reversed,
Where age becomes the handsome child at last,
The glass sea parted for the country sailors.

There move the enormous comics, drawn from life—
My father as an Airedale and a gardener,
My mother chasing letters with a knife.
You are not present as a character;
(Only the family have speaking parts).
You are a valley or a river-bend,
The one an aunt refers to as a friend,
The tree from which the weasel racing starts.

Behind me roars the other world it matches,
Love's daytime kingdom which I say you rule,
His total state where all must wear your badges
Keep order perfect as a naval school.
Noble emotions, organized and massed,
Line the straight flood-lit tracks of memory
To cheer your image as it flashes by,
All lust at once informed on and suppressed.

Yours is the only name expressive there,
And family affection speaks in cypher.

Lay-out of hospital and street and square
That comfort to its homesick children offer,
As I, their author, stand between these dreams,
Unable to choose either for a home,
Your would-be lover who has never come
In the great bed at midnight to your arms.

Such dreams are amorous; they are indeed:
But no one but myself is loved in these,
While time flies on above the dreamer's head
Flies on, flies on, and with your beauty flies,
And pride succeeds to each succeeding state,
Still able to buy up the life within,
License no liberty except his own,
Order the fireworks after the defeat.

Language of moderation cannot hide:
My sea is empty and its waves are rough;
Gone from the map the shore where childhood played,
Tight-fisted as a peasant, eating love;
Lost in my wake the archipelago,
Islands of self through which I sailed all day
Planting a pirate's flag, a generous boy;
And lost the way to action and to you.

Lost if I steer. Tempest and tide may blow
Sailor and ship past the illusive reef,
And I yet land to celebrate with you
The birth of natural order and true love:
With you enjoy the untransfigured scene,
My father down the garden in his gaiters,
My mother at her bureau writing letters,
Free to our favours, all our titles gone.

The Watchers

Now from my window-sill I watch the night,
The church clock's yellow face, the green pier light
Burn for a new imprudent year;
The silence buzzes in my ear;
The lights of near-by families are out.

Under the darkness nothing seems to stir;
The lilac bush like a conspirator
Shams dead upon the lawn, and there
Above the flagstaff the Great Bear
Hangs as a portent over Helensburgh.

O Lords of Limit, training dark and light
And setting a tabu 'twixt left and right,
The influential quiet twins
From whom all property begins,
Look leniently upon us all to-night.

No one has seen you: none can say; 'Of late—
Here, You can see the marks—They lay in wait,'
But in my thoughts to-night you seem
Forms which I saw once in a dream,
The stocky keepers of a wild estate.

With guns beneath your arms, in sun and wet,
At doorways posted or on ridges set,
By copse or bridge we know you there
Whose sleepless presences endear
Our peace to us with a perpetual threat.

Look not too closely, be not over-quick;
We have no invitation, but we are sick,
Using the mole's device, the carriage
Of peacock or rat's desperate courage,
And we shall only pass you by a trick.

Deeper towards the summer the year moves on.
What if the starving visionary have seen
 The carnival within our gates,
 Your bodies kicked about the streets,
We need your power still: use it, that none,

O, from their tables break uncontrollably away,
Lunging, insensible to injury,
 Dangerous in a room or out wild-
 -ly spinning like a top in the field,
Mopping and mowing through the sleepless day.

Journey to Iceland

And the traveller hopes: 'Let me be far from any
Physician'; and the ports have names for the sea,
 The citiless, the corroding, the sorrow;
 And North means to all: 'Reject.'

And the great plains are forever where the cold fish is hunted,
And everywhere; the light birds flicker and flaunt;
 Under the scolding flag the lover
 Of islands may see at last,

Faintly, his limited hope, as he nears the glitter
Of glaciers, the sterile immature mountains intense
 In the abnormal day of this world, and a river's
 Fan-like polyp of sand.

Then let the good citizen here find natural marvels:
A horse-shoe ravine, an issue of steam from a cleft
 In the rock, and rocks, and waterfalls brushing the
 Rocks, and among the rocks birds.

And the student of prose and conduct places to visit:
The site of a church where a bishop was put in a bag,
   The bath of a great historian, the fort where
   An outlaw dreaded the dark;

Remember the doomed man thrown by his horse and crying,
'Beautiful is the hillside, I will not go,'
   The old woman confessing, 'He that I loved the
   Best, to him I was worst.'

For Europe is absent: this is an island and therefore
A refuge, where the fast affections of its dead may be bought
   By those whose dreams accuse them of being
   Spitefully alive, and the pale

From too much passion of kissing feel pure in its deserts.
Can they? For the world is, and the present, and the lie.
   The narrow bridge over the torrent,
   And the small farm under the crag

Are the natural setting for the jealousies of a province;
And the weak vow of fidelity is formed by the cairn;
   And within the indigenous figure on horseback
   On the bridle path down by the lake

The blood moves also by crooked and furtive inches,
Asks all our questions: 'Where is the homage? When
   Shall justice be done? O who is against me?
   Why am I always alone?'

No, our time has no favourite suburb; no local features
Are those of the young for whom all wish to care;
   The promise is only a promise, the fabulous
   Country impartially far.

Tears fall in all the rivers. Again the driver
Pulls on his gloves and in a blinding snowstorm starts
   Upon his deadly journey, and again the writer
   Runs howling to his art.

The Dead Echo

'O who can ever gaze his fill,'
   Farmer and fisherman say,
'On native shore and local hill,
Grudge aching limb or callus on the hand?
Fathers, grandfathers stood upon this land,
And here the pilgrims from our loins shall stand.
   So farmer and fisherman say
   In their fortunate heyday:
   But Death's soft answer drifts across
   Empty catch or harvest loss
     Or an unlucky May.
The earth is an oyster with nothing inside it,
   Not to be born is the best for man;
The end of toil is a bailiff's order,
   Throw down the mattock and dance while you can.

'O life's too short for friends who share,'
   Travellers think in their hearts,
'The city's common bed, the air,
The mountain bivouac and the bathing beach,
Where incidents draw every day from each
Memorable gesture and witty speech.'
   So travellers think in their hearts,
   Till malice or circumstance parts
   Them from their constant humour:

And slyly Death's coercive rumour
    In the silence starts.
A friend is the old old tale of Narcissus,
    Not to be born is the best for man;
An active partner in something disgraceful,
    Change your partner, dance while you can.

'O stretch your hands across the sea,'
    The impassioned lover cries,
'Stretch them towards your harm and me.
Our grass is green, and sensual our brief bed,
The stream sings at its foot, and at its head
The mild and vegetarian beasts are fed.'
    So the impassioned lover cries
    Till his storm of pleasure dies:
    From the bedpost and the rocks
    Death's enticing echo mocks,
        And his voice replies.
The greater the love, the more false to its object,
    Not to be born is the best for man;
After the kiss comes the impulse to throttle,
    Break the embraces, dance while you can.

'I see the guilty world forgiven,'
    Dreamer and drunkard sing,
'The ladders let down out of heaven,
The laurels springing from the martyrs' blood,
The children skipping where the weepers stood,
The lovers natural and the beasts all good.'
    So dreamer and drunkard sing
    Till day their sobriety bring:
    Parrotwise with death's reply
    From whelping fear and nesting lie,
        Woods and their echoes ring.
The desires of the heart are as crooked as corkscrews,
    Not to be born is the best for man;

The second-best is a formal order,
    The dance's pattern; Dance while you can.
Dance, dance, for the figure is easy,
    The tune is catching and will not stop;
Dance till the stars come down with the rafters:
    Dance, dance, dance till you drop.

from *New Year Letter*

Whenever I begin to think
About the human creature we
Must nurse to sense and decency,
An English area comes to mind,
I see the native of my kind
As a locality I love,
The limestone moors that stretch from *Brough*
To *Hexham* and the *Roman Wall*,
There is my symbol of us all.
There, where the *Eden* leisures through
Its sandstone valley, is my view
Of green and civil life that dwells
Below a cliff of savage fells
From which original address
Man faulted into consciousness.
Along the line of lapse the fire
Of life's impersonal desire
Burst through his sedentary rock
And, as at *Dufton* and at *Knock*,
Thrust up between his mind and heart
Enormous cones of myth and art.
Always my boy of wish returns
To those peat-stained deserted burns
That feed the *Wear* and *Tyne* and *Tees*
And, turning states to strata, sees

How basalt long oppressed broke out
In wild revolt at *Cauldron Snout*
And from the relics of old mines
Derives his algebraic signs
For all in man that mourns and seeks,
For all of his renounced techniques
Their tramways overgrown with grass,
For lost belief, for all Alas
The derelict lead-smelting mill
Flued to its chimney up the hill
That smokes no answer any more
But points, a landmark on *Bolts Law*,
The finger of all question. There
In *Rookhope* I was first aware
Of Self and Not-self, Death and Dread:
Adits were entrances which led
Down to the Outlawed, to the Others,
The Terrible, the Merciful, the Mothers;
Alone in the hot day I knelt
Upon the edge of shafts and felt
The deep *Urmutterfurcht* that drives
Us into knowledge all our lives,
The far interior of our fate
To civilize and to create
Das Weibliche that bids us come
To find what we're escaping from.
There I dropped pebbles, listened, heard
The reservoir of darkness stirred;
'*O deine Mutter kehrt dir nicht*
Wieder. Du selbst bin ich, dein' Pflicht
Und Liebe. Brach sie nur mein Bild.'
And I was conscious of my guilt.

Atlantis

Being set on the idea
    Of getting to Atlantis,
You have discovered of course
    Only the Ship of Fools is
Making the voyage this year,
As gales of abnormal force
    Are predicted, and that you
    Must, therefore, be ready to
Behave absurdly enough
    To pass for one of The Boys,
At least appearing to love
    Hard liquor, horseplay and noise.

Should storms, as may well happen,
    Drive you to anchor a week
In some old harbour-city
    Of Ionia, then speak
With her witty scholars, men
Who have proved there cannot be
    Such a place as Atlantis:
    Learn their logic, but notice
How its subtlety betrays
    Their enormous simple grief;
Thus they shall teach you the ways
    To doubt that you may believe.

If, later, you run aground
    Among the headlands of Thrace,
Where with torches all night long
    A naked barbaric race
Leaps frenziedly to the sound
Of conch and dissonant gong;
    On that stony savage shore
    Strip off your clothes and dance, for

Unless you are capable
  Of forgetting completely
About Atlantis, you will
  Never finish your journey.

Again, should you come to gay
  Carthage or Corinth, take part
In their endless gaiety;
  And if in some bar a tart,
As she strokes your hair, should say
'This is Atlantis, dearie,'
  Listen with attentiveness
  To her life-story: unless
You become acquainted now
  With each refuge that tries to
Counterfeit Atlantis, how
  Will you recognize the true?

Assuming you beach at last
  Near Atlantis, and begin
The terrible trek inland
  Through squalid woods and frozen
Tundras where all are soon lost;
If, forsaken then, you stand,
  Dismissal everywhere,
  Stone and snow, silence and air,
O remember the great dead
  And honour the fate you are,
Travelling and tormented,
  Dialectic and bizarre.

Stagger onward rejoicing;
  And even then if, perhaps
Having actually got
  To the last col, you collapse
With all Atlantis shining

Below you yet you cannot
   Descend, you should still be proud
Just to peep at Atlantis
   In a poetic vision:
Give thanks and lie down in peace,
   Having seen your salvation.

All the little household gods
   Have started crying, but say
Good-bye now, and put to sea.
   Farewell, dear friend, farewell: may
Hermes, master of the roads
And the four dwarf Kabiri,
   Protect and serve you always;
   And may the Ancient of Days
Provide for all you must do
   His invisible guidance,
Lifting up, friend, upon you
   The light of His countenance.

from *The Age of Anxiety*

(a)   Let us then
Consider rather the incessant Now of
The traveller through time, his tired mind
Biased towards bigness since his body must
Exaggerate to exist, possessed by hope,
Acquisities, in quest of his own
Absconded self yet scared to find it
As he bumbles by from birth to death
Menaced by madness; whose mode of being,
Bashful or braggart, is to be at once
Outside and inside his own demand
For personal pattern. His pure I

Must give account of and greet his Me,
That field of force where he feels he thinks,
His past present, presupposing death,
Must ask what he is in order to be
And make meaning by omission and stress,
Avid of elseness. All that exists
Matters to man; he minds what happens
And feels he is at fault, a fallen soul
With power to place, to explain every
What in his world but why he is neither
God nor good, this guilt his insoluble
Final fact, infusing his private
Nexus of needs, his noted aims with
Incomprehensible comprehensive dread
At not being what he knows that before
This world was he was willed to become.

(b)   As I pull on my gloves and prepare
For another day-long drive,
The landscape is full of life:
Nieces of millionaires
Twitter on terraces,
Peasant wives are pounding
Linen on stones by a stream,
And a doctor's silk hat dances
On top of a hedge as he hurries
Along a sunken lane.

All these and theirs are at home,
May love or hate their age
And the beds they are built to fit;
Only I have no work
But my endless journey, its joy
The whirr of wheels, the hiss
As moonlit miles flash by,
Its grief the glimpse of a face

67

Whose unique beauty cannot
Be asked to alter with me.

Or must everyone see himself
As I, as the pilgrim prince
Whose life belongs to his quest
For the Truth, the tall princess,
The buried gold or the Grail,
The important thought-of Thing
Which is never here and now
Like this world through which he goes
That all the others appear
To possess the secret of?

In Praise of Limestone

If it form the one landscape that we the inconstant ones
    Are consistently homesick for, this is chiefly
Because it dissolves in water. Mark these rounded slopes
    With their surface fragrance of thyme and beneath
A secret system of caves and conduits; hear these springs
    That spurt out everywhere with a chuckle
Each filling a private pool for its fish and carving
    Its own little ravine whose cliffs entertain
The butterfly and the lizard; examine this region
    Of short distances and definite places:
What could be more like Mother or a fitter background
    For her son, the flirtatious male who lounges
Against a rock in the sunlight, never doubting
    That for all his faults he is loved; whose works are but
Extensions of his power to charm? From weathered outcrop
    To hill-top temple, from appearing water to
Conspicuous fountains, from a wild to a formal vineyard,
    Are ingenious but short steps that a child's wish

To receive more attention than his brothers, whether
    By pleasing or teasing, can easily take.

Watch, then, the band of rivals as they climb up and down
    Their steep stone gennels in twos and threes, sometimes
Arm in arm, but never, thank God, in step; or engaged
    On the shady side of a square at midday in
Voluble discourse, knowing each other too well to think
    There are any important secrets, unable
To conceive a god whose temper-tantrums are moral
    And not to be pacified by a clever line
Or a good lay: for, accustomed to a stone that responds,
    They have never had to veil their faces in awe
Of a crater whose blazing fury could not be fixed;
    Adjusted to the local needs of valleys
Where everything can be touched or reached by walking,
    Their eyes have never looked into infinite space
Through the lattice-work of a nomad's comb; born lucky,
    Their legs have never encountered the fungi
And insects of the jungle, the monstrous forms and lives
    With which we have nothing, we like to hope, in common.
So, when one of them goes to the bad, the way his mind
            works
    Remains comprehensible: to become a pimp
Or deal in fake jewellery or ruin a fine tenor voice
    For effects that bring down the house could happen to all
But the best and the worst of us . . .
                            That is why, I suppose,
    The best and worst never stayed here long but sought
Immoderate soils where the beauty was not so external,
    The light less public and the meaning of life
Something more than a mad camp. 'Come!' cried the granite
            wastes,
    'How evasive is your humour, how accidental
Your kindest kiss, how permanent is death.' (Saints-to-be
    Slipped away sighing.) 'Come!' purred the clays and gravels.

'On our plains there is room for armies to drill; rivers
   Wait to be tamed and slaves to construct you a tomb
In the grand manner: soft as the earth is mankind and both
   Need to be altered.' (Intendent Caesars rose and
Left, slamming the door.) But the really reckless were fetched
   By an older colder voice, the oceanic whisper:
'I am the solitude that asks and promises nothing;
   That is how I shall set you free. There is no love;
There are only the various envies, all of them sad.'

They were right, my dear, all those voices were right
And still are; this land is not the sweet home that it looks,
   Nor its peace the historical calm of a site
Where something was settled once and for all: a backward
   And dilapidated province, connected
To the big busy world by a tunnel, with a certain
   Seedy appeal, is that all it is now? Not quite:
It has a worldly duty which in spite of itself
   It does not neglect, but calls into question
All the Great Powers assume; it disturbs our rights. The poet,
   Admired for his earnest habit of calling
The sun the sun, his mind Puzzle, is made uneasy
   By these solid statues which so obviously doubt
His antimythological myth; and these gamins,
   Pursuing the scientist down the tiled colonnade
With such lively offers, rebuke his concern for Nature's
   Remotest aspects: I, too, am reproached, for what
And how much you know. Not to lose time, not to get
      caught,
   Not to be left behind, not, please! to resemble
The beasts who repeat themselves, or a thing like water
   Or stone whose conduct can be predicted, these
Are our Common Prayer, whose greatest comfort is music
   Which can be made anywhere, is invisible,
And does not smell. In so far as we have to look forward
   To death as a fact, no doubt we are right: but if

Sins can be forgiven, if bodies rise from the dead,
    These modifications of matter into
Innocent athletes and gesticulating fountains,
    Made solely for pleasure, make a further point:
The blessed will not care what angle they are regarded from,
    Having nothing to hide. Dear, I know nothing of
Either, but when I try to imagine a faultless love
    Or the life to come, what I hear is the murmur
Of underground streams, what I see is a limestone landscape.

Plains

For Wendell Johnson

I can imagine quite easily ending up
    In a decaying port on a desolate coast,
Cadging drinks from the unwary, a quarrelsome,
    Disreputable old man; I can picture
A second childhood in a valley, scribbling
    Reams of edifying and unreadable verse;
But I cannot see a plain without a shudder:
    'O God, please, please, don't ever make me live there!'

It's horrible to think what peaks come down to,
    That pecking rain and squelching glacier defeat
Tall pomps of stone where goddesses lay sleeping,
    Dreaming of being woken by some chisel's kiss,
That what those blind brutes leave when they are through is
                nothing
    But a mere substance, a clay that meekly takes
The potter's cuff, a gravel that as concrete
    Will unsex any space which it encloses.

And think of growing where all elsewheres are equal!
    So long as there's a hill-ridge somewhere the dreamer

Can place his land of marvels; in poor valleys
    Orphans can head downstream to seek a million:
Here nothing points; to choose between Art and Science
    An embryo genius would have to spin a stick.
What could these farms do if set loose but drift like clouds,
    What goal of unrest is there but the Navy?

Romance? Not in this weather. Ovid's charmer
    Who leads the quadrilles in Arcady, boy-lord
Of hearts who can call their Yes and No their own,
    Would, madcap that he is, soon die of cold or sunstroke:
These lives are in firmer hands; that old grim She
    Who makes the blind dates for the hatless genera
Creates their country matters. (Woe to the child-bed,
    Woe to the strawberries, if She's in Her moods!)

And on these attend, greedy as fowl and harsher
    Than any climate, Caesar with all his They.
If a tax-collector disappear in the hills,
    If, now and then, a keeper is shot in the forest,
No thunder follows, but where roads run level,
    How swift to the point of protest strides the Crown.
It hangs, it flogs, it fines, it goes. There is drink.
    There are wives to beat. But Zeus is with the strong.

Born as a rule in some small place (an island,
    Quite often, where a smart lad can spot the bluff
Whence cannon would put the harbour at his mercy),
    Though it is here they chamber with Clio. At this brook
The Christian cross-bow stopped the Heathen scimitar;
    Here is a windmill whence an emperor saw
His right wing crumple; across these cabbage fields
    A pretender's Light Horse made their final charge.

If I were a plainsman I should hate us all,
    From the mechanic rioting for a cheap loaf

To the fastidious palate, hate the painter
  Who steals my wrinkles for his Twelve Apostles,
Hate the priest who cannot even make it shower.
  What could I smile at as I trudged behind my harrow
But bloodshot images of rivers screaming,
  Marbles in panic, and Don't-Care made to care?

As it is, though, I know them personally
  Only as a landscape common to two nightmares:
Across them, spotted by spiders from afar,
  I have tried to run, knowing there was no hiding and no help;
On them, in brilliant moonlight, I have lost my way
  And stood without a shadow at the dead centre
Of an abominable desolation,
  Like Tarquin ravished by his post-coital sadness.

Which goes to show I've reason to be frightened
  Not of plains, of course, but of me. I should like
—Who wouldn't?—to shoot beautifully and be obeyed,
  (I should also like to own a cave with two exits);
I wish I weren't so silly. Though I can't pretend
  To think these flats poetic, it's as well at times
To be reminded that nothing is lovely,
  Not even in poetry, which is not the case.

Mainly the Thirties

from *Paid on Both Sides*

Chorus : The Spring unsettles sleeping partnerships,
Foundries improve their casting process, shops
Open a further wing on credit till
The winter. In summer boys grow tall
With running races on the froth-wet sand,
War is declared there, here a treaty signed;
Here a scrum breaks up like a bomb, there troops
Deploy like birds. But proudest into traps
Have fallen. These gears which ran in oil for week
By week, needing to look, now will not work;
Those manors mortgaged twice to pay for love
Go to another.
          O how shall man live
Whose thought is born, child of one farcical night,
To find him old? The body warm but not
By choice, he dreams of folk in dancing bunches,
Of tart wine spilt on home-made benches,
Where learns, one drawn apart, a secret will
Restore the dead; but comes thence to a wall.
Outside on frozen soil lie armies killed
Who seem familiar but they are cold.
Now the most solid wish he tries to keep
His hands show through; he never will look up,
Say 'I am good'. On him misfortune falls
More than enough. Better where no one feels,
The out-of-sight, buried too deep for shafts.

77

The Questioner Who Sits So Sly

Will you turn a deaf ear
To what they said on the shore,
Interrogate their poises
In their rich houses;

Of stork-legged heaven-reachers
Of the compulsory touchers
The sensitive amusers
And masked amazers?

Yet wear no ruffian badge
Nor lie behind the hedge
Waiting with bombs of conspiracy
In arm-pit secrecy;

Carry no talisman
For germ or the abrupt pain
Needing no concrete shelter
Nor porcelain filter?

Will you wheel death anywhere
In his invalid chair,
With no affectionate instant
But his attendant?

For to be held for friend
By an undeveloped mind
To be joke for children is
Death's happiness:

Whose anecdotes betray
His favourite colour as blue
Colour of distant bells
And boy's overalls.

His tales of the bad lands
Disturb the sewing hands;
Hard to be superior
On parting nausea;

To accept the cushions from
Women against martyrdom.
Yet applauding the circuits
Of racing cyclists.

Never to make signs
Fear neither maelstrom nor zones
Salute with soldiers' wives
When the flag waves;

Remembering there is
No recognized gift for this;
No income, no bounty,
No promised country.

But to see brave sent home
Hermetically sealed with shame
And cold's victorious wrestle
With molten metal.

A neutralizing peace
And an average disgrace
Are honour to discover
For later other.

A Free One

Watch any day his nonchalant pauses, see
His dextrous handling of a wrap as he
Steps after into cars, the beggar's envy.

'There is a free one,' many say, but err.
He is not that returning conqueror,
Nor ever the poles' circumnavigator.

But poised between shocking falls on razor-edge
Has taught himself this balancing subterfuge
Of the accosting profile, the erect carriage.

The song, the varied action of the blood
Would drown the warning from the iron wood
Would cancel the inertia of the buried:

Travelling by daylight on from house to house
The longest way to the intrinsic peace,
With love's fidelity and with love's weakness.

Shut Your Eyes and Open Your Mouth

Sentries against inner and outer,
At stated interval is feature;
And how shall enemy on these
Make sudden raid or lasting peace?
For bribery were vain to try
Against the incorruptible eye
Too amply paid with tears, the chin
Has hairs to hide its weakness in,
And proud bridge and indignant nostril
Nothing to do but to look noble.
But in between these lies the mouth;
Watch that, that you may parley with:
There strategy comes easiest,
Though it seem stern, was seen compressed

Over a lathe, refusing answer,
It will release the ill-fed prisoner
It will do murder or betray
For either party equally,
Yielding at last to a close kiss
It will admit tongue's soft advance,
So longed for, given in abandon,
Given long since, had it but known.

1929

It is time for the destruction of error.
The chairs are being brought in from the garden,
The summer talk stopped on that savage coast
Before the storms, after the guests and birds:
In sanatoriums they laugh less and less,
Less certain of cure; and the loud madman
Sinks now into a more terrible calm.
The falling children know it, the children,
At play on the fuming alkali-tip
Or by the flooded football ground know it—
This is the dragon's day, the devourer's:
Orders are given to the enemy for a time
With underground proliferation of mould,
With constant whisper and the casual question,
To haunt the poisoned in his shunned house,
To destroy the efflorescence of the flesh,
The intricate play of the mind, to enforce
Conformity with the orthodox bone,
With organized fear, the articulated skeleton.
You whom I gladly walk with, touch,
Or wait for as one certain of good,
We know it, we know that love
Needs more than the admiring excitement of union,

More than the abrupt self-confident farewell,
The heel on the finishing blade of grass,
The self-confidence of the falling root,
Needs death, death of the grain, our death,
Death of the old gang; would leave them
In sullen valley where is made no friend,
The old gang to be forgotten in the spring,
The hard bitch and the riding-master,
Stiff underground; deep in clear lake
The lolling bridegroom, beautiful, there.

Consider

Consider this and in our time
As the hawk sees it or the helmeted airman:
The clouds rift suddenly—look there
At cigarette-end smouldering on a border
At the first garden party of the year.
Pass on, admire the view of the massif
Through plate-glass windows of the Sport Hotel;
Join there the insufficient units
Dangerous, easy, in furs, in uniform
And constellated at reserved tables
Supplied with feelings by an efficient band
Relayed elsewhere to farmers and their dogs
Sitting in kitchens in the stormy fens.

Long ago, supreme Antagonist,
More powerful than the great northern whale
Ancient and sorry at life's limiting defect,
In Cornwall, Mendip, or the Pennine moor
Your comments on the highborn mining-captains,
Found they no answer, made them wish to die
—Lie since in barrows out of harm.

You talk to your admirers every day
By silted harbours, derelict works,
In strangled orchards, and the silent comb
Where dogs have worried or a bird was shot.
Order the ill that they attack at once:
Visit the ports and, interrupting
The leisurely conversation in the bar
Within a stone's throw of the sunlit water,
Beckon your chosen out. Summon
Those handsome and diseased youngsters, those women
Your solitary agents in the country parishes;
And mobilize the powerful forces latent
In soils that make the farmer brutal
In the infected sinus, and the eyes of stoats.
Then, ready, start your rumour, soft
But horrifying in its capacity to disgust
Which, spreading magnified, shall come to be
A polar peril, a prodigious alarm,
Scattering the people, as torn-up paper
Rags and utensils in a sudden gust,
Seized with immeasurable neurotic dread.

Seekers after happiness, all who follow
The convolutions of your simple wish,
It is later than you think; nearer that day
Far other than that distant afternoon
Amid rustle of frocks and stamping feet
They gave the prizes to the ruined boys.
You cannot be away, then, no
Not though you pack to leave within an hour,
Escaping humming down arterial roads:
The date was yours; the prey to fugues,
Irregular breathing and alternate ascendancies
After some haunted migratory years
To disintegrate on an instant in the explosion of mania
Or lapse for ever into a classic fatigue.

Petition

Sir, no man's enemy, forgiving all
But will its negative inversion, be prodigal:
Send to us power and light, a sovereign touch
Curing the intolerable neural itch,
The exhaustion of weaning, the liar's quinsy,
And the distortions of ingrown virginity.
Prohibit sharply the rehearsed response
And gradually correct the coward's stance;
Cover in time with beams those in retreat
That, spotted, they turn though the reverse were great;
Publish each healer that in city lives
Or country houses at the end of drives;
Harrow the house of the dead; look shining at
New styles of architecture, a change of heart.

Chorus

from *The Dog Beneath the Skin*

The Summer holds: upon its glittering lake
Lie Europe and the islands; many rivers
Wrinkling its surface like a ploughman's palm.
Under the bellies of the grazing horses
On the far side of posts and bridges
The vigorous shadows dwindle; nothing wavers.
Calm at this moment the Dutch sea so shallow
That sunk St Pauls would ever show its golden cross
And still the deep water that divides us still from Norway.
We would show you at first an English village: You shall choose
  its location
Wherever your heart directs you most longingly to look; you
  are loving towards it:

Whether north to Scots Gap and Bellingham where the black
        rams defy the panting engine:
Or west to the Welsh Marches; to the lilting speech and the
        magicians' faces:
Wherever you were a child or had your first affair
There it stands amidst your darling scenery:
A parish bounded by the wreckers' cliff; or meadows where
        browse the Shorthorn and the maplike Frisian
As at Trent Junction where the Soar comes gliding; out of green
        Leicestershire to swell the ampler current.

Hiker with sunburn blisters on your office pallor,
Cross-country champion with corks in your hands,
When you have eaten your sandwich, your salt and your apple,
When you have begged your glass of milk from the ill-kept
        farm,
  What is it you see?

I see barns falling, fences broken,
Pasture not ploughland, weeds not wheat.
The great houses remain but only half are inhabited,
Dusty the gunrooms and the stable clocks stationary.
Some have been turned into prep-schools where the diet is in
        the hands of an experienced matron,
Others into club-houses for the golf-bore and the top-hole.
Those who sang in the inns at evening have departed; they saw
        their hope in another country,
Their children have entered the service of the suburban areas;
        they have become typists, mannequins and factory
        operatives; they desired a different rhythm of life.

But their places are taken by another population, with views
        about nature,
Brought in charabanc and saloon along arterial roads;
Tourists to whom the Tudor cafés
Offer Bovril and buns upon Breton ware

With leather work as a sideline: Filling stations
Supplying petrol from rustic pumps.

Those who fancy themselves as foxes or desire a special setting
        for spooning
Erect their villas at the right places,
Airtight, lighted, elaborately warmed;
And nervous people who will never marry
Live upon dividends in the old-world cottages
With an animal for friend or a volume of memoirs.

Man is changed by his living; but not fast enough.
His concern to-day is for that which yesterday did not occur.
In the hour of the Blue Bird and the Bristol Bomber, his
        thoughts are appropriate to the years of the Penny
        Farthing:
He tosses at night who at noonday found no truth.

The Witnesses

You are the town and we are the clock.
We are the guardians of the gate in the rock.
The Two.
On your left and on your right
In the day and in the night,
We are watching you.

Wiser not to ask just what has occurred
To them who disobeyed our word;
    To those
We were the whirlpool, we were the reef,
We were the formal nightmare, grief
    And the unlucky rose.

Climb up the crane, learn the sailor's words
When the ships from the islands laden with birds
   Come in.
Tell your stories of fishing and other men's wives:
The expansive moments of constricted lives
   In the lighted inn.

But do not imagine we do not know
Nor that what you hide with such care won't show
   At a glance.
Nothing is done, nothing is said,
But don't make the mistake of believing us dead:
   I shouldn't dance.

We're afraid in that case you'll have a fall.
We've been watching you over the garden wall
   For hours.
The sky is darkening like a stain,
Something is going to fall like rain
   And it won't be flowers.

When the green field comes off like a lid
Revealing what was much better hid:
   Unpleasant.
And look, behind you without a sound
The woods have come up and are standing round
   In deadly crescent.

The bolt is sliding in its groove,
Outside the window is the black remov-
   ers van.
And now with sudden swift emergence
Come the woman in dark glasses and the humpbacked surgeons
   And the scissor man.

This might happen any day
So be careful what you say
   Or do.

Be clean, be tidy, oil the lock,
Trim the garden, wind the clock,
Remember the Two.

Perhaps

O Love, the interest itself in thoughtless Heaven,
Make simpler daily the beating of man's heart; within,
There in the ring where name and image meet,

Inspire them with such a longing as will make his thought
Alive like patterns a murmuration of starlings,
Rising in joy over wolds, unwittingly weave.

Here too on our little reef display your power,
This fortress perched on the edge of the Atlantic scarp,
The mote between all Europe and the exile-crowded sea;

And make us as *Newton* was who, in his garden watching
The apple falling towards *England*, became aware
Between himself and her of an eternal tie.

For now that dream which so long had contented our will,
I mean, of uniting the dead into a splendid empire,
Under whose fertilizing flood the *Lancashire* moss

Sprouted up chimneys, and *Glamorgan* hid a life
Grim as a tidal rock-pool's in its glove-shaped valleys
Is already retreating into her maternal shadow;

Leaving the furnaces gasping in the impossible air,
That flotsam at which *Dumbarton* gapes and hungers;
While upon wind-loved *Rowley* no hammer shakes

The cluster of mounds like a midget golf-course, graves
Of some who created these intelligible dangerous marvels,
Affectionate people, but crude their sense of glory.

Far-sighted as falcons, they looked down another future;
For the seed in their loins were hostile though afraid of their
        pride,
And, tall with a shadow now, inertly wait.

In bar, in netted chicken-farm, in lighthouse,
Standing on these impoverished constricted acres,
The ladies and gentlemen apart, too much alone,

Consider the years of the measured world begun,
The barren virtuous marriage of stone and water.
Yet O, at this very moment of a hopeless sigh,

When, inland, they are thinking their thoughts but watching
        these islands
As children in *Chester* look to *Moel Fammau* to decide
On picnics by the clearness or withdrawal of her treeless
        crown.

Some possible dream, long coiled in the ammonite's slumber
Is uncurling, prepared to lay on our talk and reflection
Its military silence, its surgeon's idea of pain;

And out of the future into actual history,
As when *Merlin*, tamer of horses, and his lords to whom
Stonehenge was still a thought, the *Pillars* passed

And into the undared ocean swung north their prow,
Drives through the night and star-concealing dawn
For the virgin roadsteads of our hearts an unwavering keel.

Our Hunting Fathers

Our hunting fathers told the story
   Of the sadness of the creatures,
Pitied the limits and the lack
   Set in their finished features;
Saw in the lion's intolerant look,
Behind the quarry's dying glare,
Love raging for the personal glory
   That reason's gift would add,
The liberal appetite and power,
   The rightness of a god.

Who, nurtured in that fine tradition,
   Predicted the result,
Guessed Love by nature suited to
   The intricate ways of guilt,
That human ligaments could so
His southern gestures modify
And make it his mature ambition
   To think no thought but ours,
To hunger, work illegally,
   And be anonymous?

Who's Who

A shilling life will give you all the facts:
How Father beat him, how he ran away,
What were the struggles of his youth, what acts
Made him the greatest figure of his day:
Of how he fought, fished, hunted, worked all night,
Though giddy, climbed new mountains; named a sea:
Some of the last researchers even write
Love made him weep pints like you and me.

With all his honours on, he sighed for one
Who, say astonished critics, lived at home;
Did little jobs about the house with skill
And nothing else; could whistle; would sit still
Or potter round the garden; answered some
Of his long marvellous letters but kept none.

The Malverns

Here on the cropped grass of the narrow ridge I stand,
A fathom of earth, alive in air
Aloof as an admiral on the old rocks,
    England below me:
Eastward across the Midland plains
An express is leaving for a sailor's country;
    Westward is Wales
Where on clear evenings the retired and rich
From the french windows of their sheltered mansions
See the Sugarloaf standing, an upright sentinel
    Over Abergavenny.

When last I stood here I was not alone; happy
Each thought the other, thinking of a crime,
And England to our meditations seemed
    The perfect setting:
But now it has no innocence at all;
It is the isolation and the fear,
    The mood itself;
It is the body of the absent lover,
An image to the would-be hero of the soul,
The little area we are willing to forgive
    Upon conditions.

For private reasons I must have the truth, remember
These years have seen a boom in sorrow;

The presses of idleness issued more despair
    And it was honoured,
Gross Hunger took on more hands every month,
Erecting here and everywhere his vast
    Unnecessary workshops,
Europe grew anxious about her health,
Combines tottered, credits froze,
And business shivered in a banker's winter
    While we were kissing.

To-day no longer occupied like that, I give
The children at the open swimming pool
Lithe in their first and little beauty
    A closer look;
Follow the cramped clerk crooked at his desk
The guide in shorts pursuing flowers
    In their careers;
A digit of the crowd, would like to know
Them better whom the shops and trams are full of,
The little men and their mothers, not plain but
    Dreadfully ugly.

Deaf to the Welsh wind now, I hear arising
From lanterned gardens sloping to the river
Where saxophones are moaning for a comforter,
    From Gaumont theatres
Where fancy plays on hunger to produce
The noble robber, ideal of boys,
    And from cathedrals,
Luxury liners laden with souls,
Holding to the east their hulls of stone,
The high thin rare continuous worship
    Of the self-absorbed.

Here, which looked north before the Cambrian alignment,
Like the cupped hand of the keen excavator

Busy with bones, the memory uncovers
   The hopes of time;
Of empires stiff in their brocaded glory,
The luscious lateral blossoming of woe
   Scented, profuse;
And of intercalary ages of disorder
When, as they prayed in antres, fell
Upon the noblest in the country night
   Angel assassins.

Small birds above me have the grace of those who founded
The civilization of the delicate olive,
Learning the laws of love and sailing
   On the calm Aegean;
The hawk is the symbol of the rule by thirst,
The central state controlling the canals;
   And the blank sky
Of the womb's utter peace before
The cell, dividing, multiplieddesire,
And raised instead of death the image
   Of the reconciler.

And over the Cotswolds now the thunder mutters:
'What little of the truth you seers saw
They dared not tell you plainly but combined
   Assertion and refuge
In the common language of collective lying,
In codes of a bureau, laboratory slang
   And diplomats' French.
The relations of your lovers were, alas, pictorial;
The treasure that you stole, you lost; bad luck
It brought you, but you cannot put it back
   Now with caresses.

'Already behind your last evening hastens up
And all the customs your society has chosen

Harden themselves into the unbreakable
    Habits of death,
Has not your long affair with death
Of late become increasingly more serious;
    Do you not find
Him growing more attractive every day?
You shall go under and help him with the crops,
Be faithful to him, and to your friends
    Remain indifferent.'

The Priory clock chimes briefly and I recollect
I am expected to return alive
My will effective and my nerves in order
    To my situation.
'The poetry is in the pity,' Wilfred said,
And Kathy in her journal, 'To be rooted in life,
    That's what I want.'
These moods give no permission to be idle,
For men are changed by what they do;
And through loss and anger the hands of the unlucky
    Love one another.

A Bride in the Thirties

Easily, my dear, you move, easily your head,
And easily as through leaves of a photograph album I'm led
Through the night's delights and the day's impressions,
Past the tall tenements and the trees in the wood,
Though sombre the sixteen skies of Europe
            And the Danube flood.

Looking and loving our behaviours pass
The stones, the steels, and the polished glass;

Lucky to love the strategic railway,
The sterile farms where his looks are fed,
And in the policed unlucky city
            Lucky his bed.

He from these lands of terrifying mottoes
Makes worlds as innocent as Beatrix Potter's;
Through bankrupt countries where they mend the roads
Along the endless plains his will is,
Intent as a collector, to pursue
            His greens and lilies

Easy for him to find in your face
The pool of silence and the tower of grace,
To conjure a camera into a wishing rose;
Simple to excite in the air from a glance
The horses, the fountains, the side-drum, the trombone,
            And the dance, the dance.

Summoned by such a music from our time
Such images to audience come
As vanity cannot dispel nor bless;
Hunger and love in their variations,
Grouped invalids watching the flight of the birds,
            And single assassins,

Ten million of the desperate marching by,
Five feet, six feet, seven feet high,
Hitler and Mussolini in their wooing poses,
Churchill acknowledging the voters' greeting,
Roosevelt at the microphone, Van der Lubbe laughing,
            And our first meeting

But love except at our proposal
Will do no trick at his disposal,

Without opinions of his own performs
The programme that we think of merit,
And through our private stuff must work
His public spirit.

Certain it became while we were still incomplete
There were certain prizes for which we would
    never compete;
A choice was killed by every childish illness,
The boiling tears amid the hot-house plants,
The rigid promise fractured in the garden
    And the long aunts

And every day there bolted from the field
Desires to which we could not yield;
Fewer and clearer grew the plans,
Schemes for a life and sketches for a hatred,
And early among my interesting scrawls
    Appeared your portrait.

You stand now before me, flesh and bone
These ghosts would like to make their own.
Are they your choices? O be deaf
When hatred would proffer her immediate pleasure,
And glory swap her fascinating rubbish
    For your one treasure.

Be deaf, too, standing uncertain now,
A pine-tree shadow across your brow,
To what I hear and wish I did not,
The voice of love saying lightly, brightly—
'Be Lubbe, be Hitler, but be my good
    Daily, nightly.'

The power that corrupts, that power to excess
The beautiful quite naturally possess;

To them the fathers and the children turn,
And all who long for their destruction,
The arrogant and self-insulted, wait
                    The looked instruction.

Shall idleness ring then your eyes like the pest,
O will you, unnoticed and mildly like the rest,
Will you join the lost in their sneering circles,
Forfeit the beautiful interest and fall
Where the engaging face is the face of the betrayer
                    And the pang is all?

Wind shakes the tree; the mountains darken;
But the heart repeats though we would not hearken:
Yours is the choice to whom the gods awarded
The language of learning and the language of love,
Crooked to move as a moneybag or a cancer,
                    Or straight as a dove.

Birthday Poem

(To Christopher Isherwood)

August for the people and their favourite islands.
Daily the steamers sidle up to meet
The effusive welcome of the pier, and soon
The luxuriant life of the steep stone valleys,
The sallow oval faces of the city
Begot in passion or good-natured habit,
Are caught by waiting coaches, or laid bare
Beside the undiscriminating sea.

Lulled by the light they live their dreams of freedom;
May climb the old road twisting to the moors,
Play leap frog, enter cafés, wear
The tigerish blazer and the dove-like shoe.

The yachts upon the little lake are theirs,
The gulls ask for them, and to them the band
Makes its tremendous statements; they control
The complicated apparatus of amusement.

All types that can intrigue the writer's fancy,
Or sensuality approves, are here.
And I, each meal-time with the families,
The animal brother and his serious sister,
Or after breakfast on the urned steps watching
The defeated and disfigured marching by,
Have thought of you, Christopher, and wished beside me
Your squat spruce body and enormous head.

Nine years ago, upon that southern island
Where the wild Tennyson became a fossil,
Half-boys, we spoke of books and praised
The acid and austere, behind us only
The stuccoed suburb and expensive school.
Scented our turf, the distant baying
Nice decoration to the artist's wish;
Yet fast the deer was flying through the wood.

Our hopes were set still on the spies' career,
Prizing the glasses and the old felt hat,
And all the secrets we discovered were
Extraordinary and false; for this one coughed
And it was gasworks coke, and that one laughed
And it was snow in bedrooms; many wore wigs,
The coastguard signalled messages of love,
The enemy were sighted from the Norman tower.

Five summers pass and now we watch
The Baltic from a balcony: the word is love.
Surely one fearless kiss would cure
The million fevers, a stroking brush

The insensitive refuse from the burning core.
Was there a dragon who had closed the works
While the starved city fed it with the Jews?
Then love would tame it with his trainer's look.

Pardon the studied taste that could refuse
The golf-house quick one and the rector's tea;
Pardon the nerves the thrushes could not soothe,
Yet answered promptly the no-subtler lure
To private joking in a panelled room,
The solitary vitality of tramps and madmen;
Believed the whisper in the double bed:
Pardon for these and every flabby fancy.

For now the moulding images of growth
That made our interest and us, are gone.
Louder to-day the wireless roars
Warnings and lies, and it is little comfort
Among the well-shaped cosily to flit,
Or longer to desire about our lives
The beautiful loneliness of the banks, or find
The stoves and resignations of the frozen plains.

The close-set eyes of mother's boy
Saw nothing to be done; we look again:
See Scandal praying with her sharp knees up,
And Virtue stood at Weeping Cross,
The green thumb to the ledger knuckled down,
And Courage to his leaking ship appointed,
Slim Truth dismissed without a character,
And gaga Falsehood highly recommended.

Greed showing shamelessly her naked money,
And all Love's wondering eloquence debased
To a collector's slang, Smartness in furs,
And Beauty scratching miserably for food,

Honour self-sacrificed for Calculation,
And Reason stoned by Mediocrity,
Freedom by Power shockingly maltreated,
And Justice exiled till Saint Geoffrey's Day.

So in this hour of crisis and dismay,
What better than your strict and adult pen
Can warn us from the colours and the consolations,
The showy arid works, reveal
The squalid shadow of academy and garden,
Make action urgent and its nature clear?
Who give us nearer insight to resist
The expanding fear, the savaging disaster?

This then my birthday wish for you, as now
From the narrow window of my fourth floor room
I smoke into the night, and watch reflections
Stretch in the harbour. In the houses
The little pianos are closed, and a clock strikes.
And all sway forward on the dangerous flood
Of history, that never sleeps or dies,
And, held one moment, burns the hand.

Macao

A weed from Catholic Europe, it took root
Between the yellow mountains and the sea,
And bore these gay stone houses like a fruit,
And grew on China imperceptibly.

Rococo images of Saint and Saviour
Promise her gamblers fortunes when they die;
Churches beside the brothels testify
That faith can pardon natural behaviour.

This city of indulgence need not fear
The major sins by which the heart is killed,
And governments and men are torn to pieces:

Religious clocks will strike; the childish vices
Will safeguard the low virtues of the child;
And nothing serious can happen here.

In Time of War: Sonnet XVI

Here war is simple like a monument:
A telephone is speaking to a man;
Flags on a map assert that troops were sent;
A boy brings milk in bowls. There is a plan

For living men in terror of their lives,
Who thirst at nine who were to thirst at noon,
And can be lost and are, and miss their wives,
And, unlike an idea, can die too soon.

But ideas can be true although men die,
And we can watch a thousand faces
Made active by one lie:

And maps can really point to places
Where life is evil now:
Nanking; Dachau.

from *Commentary* in *In Time of War*

Night falls on China; the great arc of travelling shadow
Moves over land and ocean, altering life:
Thibet already silent, the packed Indias cooling,

Inert in the paralysis of caste. And though in Africa
The vegetation still grows fiercely like the young,
And in the cities that receive the slanting radiations

The lucky are at work, and most still know they suffer
The dark will touch them soon: night's tiny noises
Will echo vivid in the owl's developed ear,

Vague in the anxious sentry's; and the moon look down
On battlefields and dead men lying, heaped like treasure,
On lovers ruined in a brief embrace, on ships

Where exiles watched the sea: and in the silence
The cry that streams out into the indifferent spaces,
And never stops or slackens, may be heard more clearly,

Above the everlasting murmur of the woods and rivers,
And more insistent than the lulling answer of the waltzes,
Or hum of printing presses turning forests into lies;

As now I hear it, rising round me from Shanghai,
And mingling with the distant mutter of guerrilla fighting,
The voice of Man: 'O teach us to outgrow our madness.

Ruffle the perfect manners of the frozen heart,
And once again compel it to be awkward and alive,
To all it suffered once a weeping witness.

Clear from the head the masses of impressive rubbish;
Rally the lost and trembling forces of the will,
Gather them up and let them loose upon the earth,

Till, as the contribution of our star, we follow
The clear instructions of that Justice, in the shadow
Of Whose uplifting, loving, and constraining power
All human reasons, do rejoice and operate.'

Musée des Beaux Arts

About suffering they were never wrong,
The Old Masters: how well they understood
Its human position; how it takes place
While someone else is eating or opening a window or just
    walking dully along;
How, when the aged are reverently, passionately waiting
For the miraculous birth, there always must be
Children who did not specially want it to happen, skating
On a pond at the edge of the wood:
They never forgot
That even the dreadful martyrdom must run its course
Anyhow in a corner, some untidy spot
Where the dogs go on with their doggy life and the torturer's
    horse
Scratches its innocent behind on a tree.

In Brueghel's *Icarus*, for instance: how everything turns away
Quite leisurely from the disaster; the ploughman may
Have heard the splash, the forsaken cry,
But for him it was not an important failure; the sun shone
As it had to on the white legs disappearing into the green
Water; and the expensive delicate ship that must have seen
Something amazing, a boy falling out of the sky,
Had somewhere to get to and sailed calmly on.

The Composer

All the others translate: the painter sketches
A visible world to love or reject;
Rummaging into his living, the poet fetches
The images out that hurt and connect.

From Life to Art by painstaking adaption,
Relying on us to cover the rift;
Only your notes are pure contraption,
Only your song is an absolute gift.

Pour out your presence, O delight, cascading
The falls of the knee and the weirs of the spine,
Our climate of silence and doubt invading;

You alone, alone, O imaginary song,
Are unable to say an existence is wrong,
And pour out your forgiveness like a wine.

Matthew Arnold

His gift knew what he was—a dark disordered city;
Doubt hid it from the father's fond chastizing sky;
Where once the mother-farms had glowed protectively,
Stood the haphazard alleys of the neighbour's pity.

—Yet would have gladly lived in him and learned his ways,
And grown observant like a beggar, and become
Familiar with each square and boulevard and slum,
And found in the disorder a whole world to praise.

But all his homeless reverence revolted, cried:
'I am my father's forum and he shall be heard,
Nothing shall contradict his holy final word,
Nothing.' And thrust his gift in prison till it died,

And left him nothing but a jailor's voice and face,
And all rang hollow but the clear denunciation
Of a gregarious optimistic generation
That saw itself already in a father's place.

The Unknown Citizen

(To JS/07/M/378 This Marble Monument
Is Erected by the State)

He was found by the Bureau of Statistics to be
One against whom there was no official complaint,
And all the reports on his conduct agree
That, in the modern sense of an old-fashioned word, he was
      a saint,
For in everything he did he served the Great Community.
Except for the War till the day he retired
He worked in a factory and never got fired,
But satisfied his employers, Fudge Motors Inc.
Yet he wasn't a scab or odd in his views,
For his Union reports that he paid his dues,
(Our report on his Union shows it was sound)
And our Social Psychology workers found
That he was popular with his mates and liked a drink.
The Press are convinced that he bought a paper every day
And that his reactions to advertisements were normal in
      every way.
Policies taken out in his name prove that he was fully
      insured,
And his Health-card shows he was once in hospital but left it
      cured.
Both Producers Research and High-Grade Living declare
He was fully sensible to the advantages of the Instalment
      Plan
And had everything necessary to the Modern Man,
A phonograph, a radio, a car and a frigidaire.
Our researchers into Public Opinion are content
That he held the proper opinions for the time of year;
When there was peace, he was for peace; when there was
      war, he went.
He was married and added five children to the population,

Which our Eugenist says was the right number for a parent
      of his generation,
And our teachers report that he never interfered with their
      education.
Was he free? Was he happy? The question is absurd:
Had anything been wrong, we should certainly have heard.

Spain, *1937*

Yesterday all the past. The language of size
Spreading to China along the trade-routes; the diffusion
      Of the counting-frame and the cromlech;
Yesterday the shadow-reckoning in the sunny climates.

Yesterday the assessment of insurance by cards,
The divination of water; yesterday the invention
      Of cart-wheels and clocks, the taming of
Horses; yesterday the bustling world of navigators.

Yesterday the abolition of fairies and giants;
The fortress like a motionless eagle eyeing the valley,
      The chapel built in the forest;
Yesterday the carving of angels and of frightening gargoyles.

The trial of heretics among the columns of stone;
Yesterday the theological feuds in the taverns
      And the miraculous cure at the fountain;
Yesterday the Sabbath of Witches. But to-day the struggle.

Yesterday the installation of dynamos and turbines;
The construction of railways in the colonial desert;
      Yesterday the classic lecture
On the origin of Mankind. But to-day the struggle.

Yesterday the belief in the absolute value of Greek;
The fall of the curtain upon the death of a hero;
> Yesterday the prayer to the sunset,
And the adoration of madmen. But to-day the struggle.

As the poet whispers, startled among the pines
Or, where the loose waterfall sings, compact, or upright
> On the crag by the leaning tower:
'O my vision. O send me the luck of the sailor.'

And the investigator peers through his instruments
At the inhuman provinces, the virile bacillus
> Or enormous Jupiter finished:
'But the lives of my friends. I inquire, I inquire.'

And the poor in their fireless lodgings dropping the sheets
Of the evening paper: 'Our day is our loss. O show us
> History the operator, the
Organizer, Time the refreshing river.'

And the nations combine each cry, invoking the life
That shapes the individual belly and orders
> The private nocturnal terror:
'Did you not found once the city state of the sponge,

'Raise the vast military empires of the shark
And the tiger, establish the robin's plucky canton?
> Intervene, O descend as a dove or
A furious papa or a mild engineer: but descend.'

And the life, if it answers at all, replies from the heart
And the eyes and the lungs, from the shops and squares of
> the city:
> 'O no, I am not the Mover,
Not to-day, not to you. To you I'm the

'Yes-man, the bar-companion, the easily-duped:
I am whatever you do; I am your vow to be
          Good, your humorous story;
I am your business voice; I am your marriage.

'What's your proposal? To build the Just City? I will.
I agree. Or is it the suicide pact, the romantic
          Death? Very well, I accept, for
I am your choice, your decision: yes, I am Spain.'

Many have heard it on remote peninsulas,
On sleepy plains, in the aberrant fishermen's islands,
          In the corrupt heart of the city;
Have heard and migrated like gulls or the seeds of a flower.

They clung like burrs to the long expresses that lurch
Through the unjust lands, through the night, through the
          alpine tunnel;
          They floated over the oceans;
They walked the passes: they came to present their lives.

On that arid square, that fragment nipped off from hot
Africa, soldered so crudely to inventive Europe,
          On that tableland scored by rivers,
Our fever's menacing shapes are precise and alive.

To-morrow, perhaps, the future: the research on fatigue
And the movements of packers; the gradual exploring of all the
          Octaves of radiation;
To-morrow the enlarging of consciousness by diet and
          breathing.

To-morrow the rediscovery of romantic love;
The photographing of ravens; all the fun under
          Liberty's masterful shadow;
To-morrow the hour of the pageant-master and the musician.

To-morrow, for the young, the poets exploding like bombs,
The walks by the lake, the winter of perfect communion;
      To-morrow the bicycle races
Through the suburbs on summer evenings: but to-day the
    struggle.

To-day the inevitable increase in the chances of death;
The conscious acceptance of guilt in the fact of murder;
      To-day the expending of powers
On the flat ephemeral pamphlet and the boring meeting.

To-day the makeshift consolations; the shared cigarette;
The cards in the candle-lit barn and the scraping concert,
      The masculine jokes; to-day the
Fumbled and unsatisfactory embrace before hurting.

The stars are dead; the animals will not look:
We are left alone with our day, and the time is short and
      History to the defeated
May say Alas but cannot help or pardon.

In Memory of W. B. Yeats

(d. Jan. 1939)

I

He disappeared in the dead of winter:
The brooks were frozen, the airports almost deserted,
And snow disfigured the public statues;
The mercury sank in the mouth of the dying day.
What instruments we have agree
The day of his death was a dark cold day.

Far from his illness
The wolves ran on through the evergreen forests,
The peasant river was untempted by the fashionable quays;
By mourning tongues
The death of the poet was kept from his poems.

But for him it was his last afternoon as himself,
An afternoon of nurses and rumours;
The provinces of his body revolted,
The squares of his mind were empty,
Silence invaded the suburbs,
The current of his feeling failed; he became his admirers.

Now he is scattered among a hundred cities
And wholly given over to unfamiliar affections;
To fiind hs happiness in another kind of wood
And be punished under a foreign code of conscience.
The words of a dead man
Are modified in the guts of the living.

But in the importance and noise of to-morrow
When the brokers are roaring like beasts on the floor of the
        Bourse,
And the poor have the sufferings to which they are fairly
        accustomed,
And each in the cell of himself is almost convinced of his
        freedom,
A few thousand will think of this day
As one thinks of a day when one did something slightly unusual.
What instruments we have agree
The day of his death was a dark cold day.

II

You were silly like us; your gift survived it all;
The parish of rich women, physical decay,

Yourself: mad Ireland hurt you into poetry.
Now Ireland has her madness and her weather still,
For poetry makes nothing happen: it survives
In the valley of its saying where executives
Would never want to tamper; it flows south
From ranches of isolation and the busy griefs,
Raw towns that we believe and die in; it survives,
A way of happening, a mouth.

III

Earth, receive an honoured guest:
William Yeats is laid to rest.
Let the Irish vessel lie
Emptied of its poetry.

In the nightmare of the dark
All the dogs of Europe bark,
And the living nations wait,
Each sequestered in its hate;

Intellectual disgrace
Stares from every human face,
And the seas of pity lie
Locked and frozen in each eye.

Follow, poet, follow right
To the bottom of the night,
With your unconstraining voice
Still persuade us to rejoice;

With the farming of a verse
Make a vineyard of the curse,
Sing of human unsuccess
In a rapture of distress;

In the deserts of the heart
Let the healing fountain start,
In the prison of his days
Teach the free man how to praise.

1st September 1939

I sit in one of the dives
On Fifty-second Street
Uncertain and afraid
As the clever hopes expire
Of a low dishonest decade:
Waves of anger and fear
Circulate over the bright
And darkened lands of the earth,
Obsessing our private lives;
The unmentionable odour of death
Offends the September night.

Accurate scholarship can
Unearth the whole offence
From Luther until now
That has driven a culture mad,
Find what occurred at Linz,
What huge imago made
A psychopathic god:
I and the public know
What all schoolchildren learn,
Those to whom evil is done
Do evil in return.

Exiled Thucydides knew
All that a speech can say
About Democracy,
And what dictators do,

The elderly rubbish they talk
To an apathetic grave;
Analysed all in his book,
The enlightenment driven away,
The habit-forming pain,
Mismanagement and grief:
We must suffer them all again.

Into this neutral air
Where blind skyscrapers use
Their full height to proclaim
The strength of Collective Man,
Each language pours its vain
Competitive excuse:
But who can live for long
In an euphoric dream;
Out of the mirror they stare,
Imperialism's face
And the international wrong.

Faces along the bar
Cling to their average day:
The lights must never go out,
The music must always play,
All the conventions conspire
To make this fort assume
The furniture of home;
Lest we should see where we are,
Lost in a haunted wood,
Children afraid of the night
Who have never been happy or good.

The windiest militant trash
Important Persons shout
Is not so crude as our wish:
What mad Nijinsky wrote

About Diaghilev
Is true of the normal heart;
For the error bred in the bone
Of each woman and each man
Craves what it cannot have,
Not universal love
But to be loved alone.

From the conservative dark
Into the ethical life
The dense commuters come,
Repeating their morning vow;
'I *will* be true to the wife,
I'll concentrate more on my work,'
And helpless governors wake
To resume their compulsory game:
Who can release them now,
Who can reach te deaf,
Who can speak fhor the dumb?

Defenceless under the night
Our world in stupor lies;
Yet, dotted everywhere,
Ironic points of light
Flash out wherever the Just
Exchange their messages:
May I, composed like them
Of Eros and of dust,
Beleaguered by the same
Negation and despair,
Show an affirming flame.

Lyrics, Songs and Musical Pieces

'What's in your mind, my dove, my coney'

What's in your mind, my dove, my coney;
Do thoughts grow like feathers, the dead end of life;
Is it making of love or counting of money,
Or raid on the jewels, the plans of a thief?

Open your eyes, my dearest dallier;
Let hunt with your hands for escaping me;
Go through the motions of exploring the familiar;
Stand on the brink of the warm white day.

Rise with the wind, my great big serpent;
Silence the birds and darken the air;
Change me with terror, alive in a moment;
Strike for the heart and have me there.

This Lunar Beauty

This lunar beauty
Has no history,
Is complete and early;
If beauty later
Bear any feature

It had a lover
And is another.

This like a dream
Keeps other time,
And daytime is
The loss of this;
For time is inches
And the heart's changes
Where ghost has haunted,
Lost and wanted.

But this was never
A ghost's endeavour
Nor, finished this,
Was ghost at ease;
And till it pass
Love shall not near
The sweetness here
Nor sorrow take
His endless look.

This One

Before this loved one
Was that one and that one
A family
And history
And ghost's adversity
Whose pleasing name
Was neighbourly shame.
Before this last one
Was much to be done,

Frontiers to cross
As clothes grew worse
And coins to pass
In a cheaper house
Before this last one
Before this loved one.

Face that the sun
Is supple on
May stir but here
Is no new year;
This gratitude for gifts is less
Than the old loss;

Touching is shaking hands
On mortgaged lands;
And smiling of
This gracious greeting
'Good day. Good luck'
Is no real meeting
But instinctive look
A backward love.

The Decoys

There are some birds in these valleys
Who flutter round the careless
With intimate appeal,
By seeming kindness trained to snaring,
They feel no falseness.

Under the spell completely
They circle can serenely,
And in the tricky light

The masked hill has a purer greenness.
Their flight looks fleeter.

Alas, the signal given,
Fingers on trigger tighten.
The real unlucky dove
Must smarting fall away from brightness,
Its love from living.

The Song of the First Mad Lady

from *The Dog Beneath the Skin*

Seen when night is silent,
The bean-shaped island
And our ugly comic servant,
Who was observant.

O the veranda and the fruit,
The tiny steamer in the bay
Startling summer with its hoot:
You have gone away.

The Two Chorus Leaders

from *The Dog Beneath the Skin*

Now through night's caressing grip
Earth and all her oceans slip,
Capes of China slide away
From her fingers into day,
And the Americas incline
Coasts towards her shadow line.

Now the ragged vagrants creep
Into crooked holes to sleep;
Just and unjust, worst and best,
Change their places as they rest;
Awkward lovers lie in fields
Where disdainful beauty yields;
While the splendid and the proud
Naked stand before the crowd,
And the losing gambler gains,
And the beggar entertains.
May sleep's healing power extend
Through these hours to each friend;
Unpursued by hostile force
Traction engine, bull or horse
Or revolting succubus;
Calmly till the morning break
Let them lie, then gently wake.

Seascape

Look, stranger, on this island now
The leaping light for your delight discovers,
Stand stable here
And silent be,
That through the channels of the ear
May wander like a river
The swaying sound of the sea.

Here at a small field's ending pause
When the chalk wall falls to the foam and its tall ledges
Oppose the pluck
And knock of the tide,
And the shingle scrambles after the suck-
ing surf,
And a gull lodges
A moment on its sheer side.

Far off like floating seeds the ships
Diverge on urgent voluntary errands,
And this full view
Indeed may enter
And move in memory as now these clouds do,
That pass the harbour mirror
And all the summer through the water saunter.

Autumn Song

Now the leaves are falling fast,
Nurse's flowers will not last;
Nurses to their graves are gone,
And the prams go rolling on.

Whispering neighbours, left and right,
Pluck us from our real delight;
And our active hands must freeze
Lonely on our separate knees.

Dead in hundreds at the back
Follow wooden in our track,
Arms raised stiffly to reprove
In false attitudes of love.

Starving through the leafless wood
Trolls run scolding for their food;
And the nightingale is dumb,
And the angel will not come.

Cold, impossible, ahead
Lifts the mountain's lovely head
Whose white waterfall could bless
Travellers in their last distress.

Underneath the Abject Willow

Underneath the abject willow,
   Lover, sulk no more:
Act from thought should quickly follow.
   What is thinking for?
Your unique and moping station
   Proves you cold;
   Stand up and fold
Your map of desolation.

Bells that toll across the meadows
   From the sombre spire
Toll for these unloving shadows
   Love does not require.
All that lives may love; why longer
   Bow to loss
   With arms across?
Strike and you shall conquer.

Geese in flocks above you flying
   Their direction know,
Brooks beneath the thin ice flowing
   To their oceans go.
Dark and dull is your distraction,
   Walk then, come,
   No longer numb
Into your satisfaction.

'Fish in the unruffled lakes'

Fish in the unruffled lakes
The swarming colours wear,

Swans in the winter air
A white perfection have,
And the great lion walks
Through his innocent grove;
Lion, fish, and swan
Act, and are gone
Upon Time's toppling wave.

We till shadowed days are done,
We must weep and sing
Duty's conscious wrong,
The Devil in the clock,
The Goodness carefully worn
For atonement or for luck;
We must lose our loves,
On each beast and bird that moves
Turn an envious look.

Sighs for folly said and done
Twist our narrow days;
But I must bless, I must praise
That you, my swan, who have
All gifts that to the swan
Impulsive Nature gave,
The majesty and pride,
Last night should add
Your voluntary love.

'O who can ever praise enough'

O who can ever praise enough
The world of his belief?
Harum-scarum childhood plays
In the meadows near his home,

In his woods love knows no wrong,
Travellers ride their placid ways,
In the cool shade of the tomb
Age's trusting footfalls ring.
O who can paint the vivid tree
And grass of phantasy?
But to create it and to guard
Shall be his whole reward:
He shall watch and he shall weep,
All his father's love deny,
To his mother's womb be lost,
Eight nights with a wanton sleep,
Then upon the ninth shall be
Bride and victim to a ghost,
And in the pit of terror thrown
Shall bear the wrath alone.

Able at Times to Cry

Wrapped in a yielding air, beside
  The flower's soundless hunger,
Close to the tree's clandestine tide,
  Close to the bird's high fever,
  Loud in his hope and anger,
Erect about his skeleton,
  Stands the expressive lover,
  Stands the deliberate man.

Beneath the hot incurious sun,
  Past stronger beasts and fairer
He picks his way, a living gun,
  With gun and lens and bible,
  A militant enquirer,

The friend, the rash, the enemy,
    The essayist, the able,
    Able at times to cry.

The friendless and unhated stone
    Lies everywhere about him,
The Bothered-One, the Not-Alone,
    The brothered and the hated
    Whose family have taught him
To set against the large and dumb,
    The timeless and the rooted,
    His money and his time.

For mother's fading hopes become
    Dull wives to his dull spirits
Soon dulled by nurse's moral thumb,
    That dullard fond betrayer,
    And, childish, he inherits,
So soon by legal father tricked,
    The tall impressive tower,
    Impressive, yes, but locked.

And ruled by dead men never met,
    By pious guess deluded,
Upon the stool of madness set
    Or stool of desolation,
    Sits murderous and clear-headed;
Enormous beauties round him move,
    For grandiose is his vision
    And grandiose his love.

Determined on Time's honest shield
    The lamb must face the tigress,
Their faithful quarrel never healed
    Though, faithless, he consider
    His dream of vaguer ages,

Hunter and victim reconciled,
　　The lion and the adder,
　　The adder and the child.

Fresh loves betray him, every day
　　Over his green horizon
A fresh deserter rides away,
　　And miles away birds mutter
　　Of ambush and of treason;
To fresh defeats he still must move,
　　To further griefs and greater,
　　And the defeat of grief.

Lullaby

Lay your sleeping head, my love,
Human on my faithless arm;
Time and fevers burn away
Individual beauty from
Thoughtful children, and the grave
Proves the child ephemeral:
But in my arms till break of day
Let the living creature lie,
Mortal, guilty, but to me
The entirely beautiful.

Soul and body have no bounds:
To lovers as they lie upon
Her tolerant enchanted slope
In their ordinary swoon,
Grave the vision Venus sends
Of supernatural sympathy,
Universal love and hope;
While an abstract insight wakes

Among the glaciers and the rocks
The hermit's sensual ecstasy.

Certainty, fidelity
On the stroke of midnight pass
Like vibrations of a bell,
And fashionable madmen raise
Their pedantic boring cry:
Every farthing of the cost,
All the dreaded cards foretell,
Shall be paid, but from this night
Not a whisper, not a thought,
Not a kiss nor look be lost.

Beauty, midnight, vision dies:
Let the winds of dawn that blow
Softly round your dreaming head
Such a day of sweetness show
Eye and knocking heart may bless,
Find the mortal world enough;
Noons of dryness see you fed
By the involuntary powers,
Nights of insult let you pass
Watched by every human love.

Orpheus

What does the song hope for? And the moved hands
A little way from the birds, the shy, the delightful?
To be bewildered and happy,
Or most of all the knowledge of life?

But the beautiful are content with the sharp notes of the air;
The warmth is enough. O if winter really
Oppose, if the weak snowflake,
What will the wish, what will the dance do?

Song

Warm are the still and lucky miles,
White shores of longing stretch away,
A light of recognition fills
   The whole great day, and bright
The tiny world of lovers' arms.

Silence invades the breathing wood
Where drowsy limbs a treasure keep,
Now greenly falls in learned shade
   Across the sleeping brows
And stirs their secret to a smile.

Restored! Returned! The lost are born
On seas of shipwreck home at last:
See! In the fire of praising burns
   The dry dumb past, and we
The life-day long shall part no more.

from *New Year Letter*

O Unicorn among the cedars
To whom no magic charm can lead us,
White childhood moving like a sigh
Through the green woods unharmed in thy
Sophisticated innocence
To call thy true love to the dance;
O Dove of science and of light
Upon the branches of the night;
O Icthus playful in the deep
Sea-lodges that for ever keep

Their secret of excitement hidden;
O sudden Wind that blows unbidden
Parting the quiet reeds; O Voice
Within the labyrinth of choice
Only the passive listener hears;
O Clock and Keeper of the years;
O Source of equity and rest,
Quando non fuerit, non est,
It without image, paradigm
Of matter, motion, number, time,
The grinning gap of Hell, the hill
Of Venus and the stairs of Will,
Disturb our negligence and chill,
Convict our pride of its offence
In all things, even penitence,
Instruct us in the civil art
Of making from the muddled heart
A desert and a city where
The thoughts that have to labour there
May find locality and peace,
And pent-up feelings their release.
Send strength sufficient for our day,
And point our knowledge on its way,
O da quod jubes, Domine.

Dear friend Elizabeth, dear friend
These days have brought me, may the end
I bring to the grave's dead-line be
More worthy of your sympathy
Than the beginning; may the truth
That no one marries lead my youth
Where you already are and bless
Me with your learned peacefulness
Who on the lives about you throw
A calm solificatio.
A warmth throughout the universe

That each for better or for worse
Must carry round with him through life,
A judge, a landscape, and a wife.
We fall down in the dance, we make
The old ridiculous mistake
But always there are such as you
Forgiving, helping what we do.
O every day in sleep and labour
Our life and death are with our neighbour
And love illuminates again
The city and the lion's den,
The world's great rage, the travel of young men.

Song for St Cecilia's Day

I

In a garden shady this holy lady
With reverent cadence and subtle psalm.
Like a black swan as death came on
Poured forth her song in perfect calm:
And by ocean's margin this innocent virgin
Constructed an organ to enlarge her prayer,
And notes tremendous from her great engine
Thundered out on the Roman air.

Blonde Aphrodite rose up excited,
Moved to delight by the melody,
White as an orchid she rode quite naked
In an oyster shell on top of the sea;
At sounds so entrancing the angels dancing
Came out of their trance into time again,
And around the wicked in Hell's abysses
The huge flame flickered and eased their pain.

Blessed Cecilia, appear in visions
To all musicians, appear and inspire:
Translated Daughter, come down and startle
Composing mortals with immortal fire.

II

I cannot grow;
I have no shadow
To run away from,
I only play.

I cannot err;
There is no creature
Whom I belong to,
Whom I could wrong.

I am defeat
When it knows it
Can now do nothing
By suffering.

All you lived through,
Dancing because you
No longer need it
For any deed.

I shall never be
Different. Love me.

III

O ear whose creatures cannot wish to fall,
O calm spaces unafraid of weight,
Where Sorrow is herself, forgetting all
The gaucheness of her adolescent state,

Where Hope within the altogether strange
From every outworn image is released,
And Dread born whole and normal like a beast
Into a world of truths that never change:
Restore our fallen day; O rearrange.

O dear white children casual as birds,
Playing among the ruined languages,
So small beside their large confusion words,
So gay against the greater silences
Of dreadful things you did: O hang the head,
Impetuous child with the tremendous brain,
O weep, child, weep, O weep away the stain,
Lost innocence who wished your lover dead,
Weep for the lives your wishes never led.

O cry created as the bow of sin
Is drawn across our trembling violin.
O weep, child, weep, O weep away the stain.
O law drummed out by hearts against the still
Long winter of our intellectual will.
That what has been may never be again,
O flute that throbs with the thanksgiving breath
Of convalescents on the shores of death.
O bless the freedom that you never chose.
O trumpets that unguarded children blow
About the fortress of their inner foe.
O wear your tribulation like a rose.

Trinculo's Song

Mechanic, merchant, king,
Are warmed by the cold clown
Whose head is in the clouds
And never can get down.

Into a solitude
Undreamed of by their fat
Quick dreams have lifted me;
The north wind steals my hat.

On clear days I can see
Green acres far below,
And the red roof where I
Was Little Trinculo.

There lies that solid world
These hands can never reach;
My history, my love,
Is but a choice of speech.

A terror shakes my tree,
A flock of words fly out,
Whereat a laughter shakes
The busy and devout.

Wild images, come down
Out of your freezing sky,
That I, like shorter men,
May get my joke and die.

Song

Deftly, admiral, cast your fly
    Into the slow deep hover,
Till the wise old trout mistake and die;
    Salt are the deeps that cover
    The glittering fleets you led,
        White is your head.

Read on, ambassador, engrossed
    In your favourite Stendhal;

The Outer Provinces are lost,
   Unshaven horsemen swill
   The great wines of the Châteaux
      Where you danced long ago.

Do not turn, do not lift, your eyes
   Toward the still pair standing
On the bridge between your properties,
   Indifferent to your minding:
   In its glory, in its power,
      This is their hour.

Nothing your strength, your skill, could do
   Can alter their embrace
Or dispersuade the Furies who
   At the appointed place
   With claw and dreadful brow
      Wait for them now.

The Duet

   All winter long the huge sad lady
Sang to her warm house of the heart betrayed:
   Love lies delirious and a-dying,
The purlieus are shaken by his sharp cry.
   But back across the fret dividing
His wildernesses from her floral side
   All winter long a scrunty beggar
With one glass eye and one hickory leg,
   Stumping about half-drunk through stony
Ravines and over dead volcanic cones,
   Refused her tragic hurt, declaring
A happy passion to the freezing air,
   Turning his barrel-organ, playing
Lanterloo, my lovely, my First-of-May.

Louder on nights when in cold glory
  The full moon made its meditative tour,
    To rich chords from her grand black piano
  She sang the disappointment and the fear
    For all her lawns and orchards: *Slowly*
The spreading ache bechills the rampant glow
  Of fortune-hunting blood, time conjures
The moskered ancestral tower to plunge
  From its fastidious cornice down to
The pigsties far below, the oaks turn brown,
  The cute little botts of the sailors
Are snapped up by the sea. But to her gale
  Of sorrow from the moonstruck darkness
That ragged runagate opposed his spark,
  For still his scrannel music-making
In tipsy joy across the gliddered lake,
  Praising for all those rocks and craters
The green refreshments of the watered state,
  Cried Nonsense to her large repining:
The windows have opened, a royal wine
  Is poured out for the subtle pudding,
Light Industry is humming in the wood
  And blue birds bless us from the fences,
We know the time and where to find our friends.

The Willow-Wren and the Stare

A starling and a willow-wren
  On a may-tree by a weir
Saw them meet and heard him say;
  'Dearest of my dear,
More lively than these waters chortling
  As they leap the dam,
My sweetest duck, my precious goose,
  My white lascivious lamb.'

With a smile she listened to him,
    Talking to her there:
What does he want? said the willow-wren;
    Much too much, said the stare.

'Forgive these loves who dwell in me,
    These brats of greed and fear,
The honking bottom-pinching clown,
    The snivelling sonneteer,
That so, between us, even these,
    Who till the grave are mine,
For all they fall so short of may,
    Dear heart, be still a sign.'
With a smile she closed her eyes,
    Silent she lay there:
Does he mean what he says? said the willow-wren;
    Some of it, said the stare.

'Hark! Wild Robin winds his horn
    And, as his notes require,
Now our laughter-loving spirits
    Must in awe retire
And let their kinder partners,
    Speechless with desire,
Go in their holy selfishness,
    Unfunny to the fire.'
Smiling, silently she threw
    Her arms about him there:
Is it only that? said the willow-wren;
    It's that as well, said the stare.

Waking in her arms he cried,
    Utterly content;
'I have heard the high good noises,
    Promoted for an instant,
Stood upon the shining outskirts
    Of that Joy I thank

For you, my dog and every goody.'
    There on the grass bank
She laughed, he laughed, they laughed together,
    Then they ate and drank:
Did he know what he meant? said the willow-wren—
    God only knows, said the stare.

Various Forms and Styles

Too Dear, Too Vague

Love by ambition
Of definition
Suffers partition
And cannot go,
From yes to no
For no is not love; no is no
The shutting of a door
The tightening jaw
A conscious sorrow;
And saying yes
Turns love into success,
Views from the rail
Of land and happiness,
Assured of all
The sofas creak
And were this all, love were
But cheek to cheek
And dear to dear.

Voices explain
Love's pleasure and love's pain,
Still tap the knee
And cannot disagree,
Hushed for aggression
Of full confession,
Likeness to likeness
Of each old weakness;

Love is not there
Love has moved to another chair.
Aware already
Of who stands next
And is not vexed
And is not giddy,
Leaves the North in place
With a good grace
And would not gather
Another to another,
Designs his own unhappiness
Foretells his own death and is faithless.

The Three Companions

'O where are you going?' said reader to rider,
'That valley is fatal when furnaces burn,
Yonder's the midden whose odours will madden,
That gap is the grave where the tall return.'

'O do you imagine,' said fearer to farer,
'That dusk will delay on your path to the pass,
Your diligent looking discover the lacking
Your footsteps feel from granite to grass?'

'O what was that bird,' said horror to hearer,
'Did you see that shape in the twisted trees?
Behind you swiftly the figure comes softly,
The spot on your skin is a shocking disease?'

'Out of this house'—said rider to reader,
'Yours never will'—said farer to fearer,
'They're looking for you'—said hearer to horror,
As he left them there, as he left them there.

The Quarry

O what is that sound which so thrills the ear
  Down in the valley drumming, drumming?
Only the scarlet soldiers, dear,
  The soldiers coming.

O what is that light I see flashing so clear
  Over the distance brightly, brightly?
Only the sun on their weapons, dear,
  As they step lightly.

O what are they doing with all that gear,
  What are they doing this morning, this morning?
Only their usual manœuvres, dear,
  Or perhaps a warning.

O why have they left the road down there,
  Why are they suddenly wheeling, wheeling?
Perhaps a change in their orders, dear.
  Why are you kneeling?

O haven't they stopped for the doctor's care,
  Haven't they reined their horses, their horses?
Why, they are none of them wounded, dear,
  None of these forces.

O is it the parson they want, with white hair,
  Is it the parson, is it, is it?
No, they are passing his gateway, dear,
  Without a visit.

O it must be the farmer who lives so near.
  It must be the farmer so cunning, so cunning?
They have passed the farmyard already, dear,
  And now they are running.

O where are you going? Stay with me here!
   Were the vows you swore deceiving, deceiving?
No, I promised to love you, dear,
   But I must be leaving.

O it's broken the lock and splintered the door,
   O it's the gate where they're turning, turning;
Their boots are heavy on the floor
   And their eyes are burning.

Song

—'O for doors to be open and an invite with gilded edges
   To dine with Lord Lobcock and Count Asthma on the
         platinum benches,
   With somersaults and fireworks, the roast and the smacking
         kisses'—
            Cried the cripples to the silent statue,
            The six beggared cripples.

—'And Garbo's and Cleopatra's wits to go astraying,
   In a feather ocean with me to go fishing and playing,
   Still jolly when the cock has burst himself with crowing'—
            Cried the cripples to the silent statue,
            The six beggared cripples.

—'And to stand on green turf among the craning yellow faces
   Dependent on the chestnut, the sable, and Arabian horses,
   And me with a magic crystal to foresee their places'—
            Cried the cripples to the silent statue,
            The six beggared cripples.

—'And this square to be deck and these pigeons sails to rig,
   And to follow the delicious breeze like a tantony pig

To the shaded feverless islands where the melons are big'—
      Cried the cripples to the silent statue,
      The six beggared cripples.

—'And these shops to be turned to tulips in a garden bed,
And me with my crutch to thrash each merchant dead
As he pokes from a flower his bald and wicked head'—
      Cried the cripples to the silent statue,
      The six beggared cripples.

—'And a hole in the bottom of heaven, and Peter and Paul
And each smug surprised saint like parachutes to fall,
And every one-legged beggar to have no legs at all'—
      Cried the cripples to the silent statue,
      The six beggared cripples.

The Sphinx

Did it once issue from the carver's hand
Healthy? Even the earliest conquerors saw
The face of a sick ape, a bandaged paw,
A Presence in the hot invaded land.

The lion of a tortured stubborn star,
It does not like the young, nor love, nor learning:
Time hurt it like a person; it lies, turning
A vast behind on shrill America,

And witnesses. The huge hurt face accuses,
And pardons nothing, least of all success.
The answers that it utters have no uses

To those who face akimbo its distress:
'Do people like me?' No. The slave amuses
The lion: 'Am I to suffer always?' Yes.

Six Sonnets from *In Time of War*

They wondered why the fruit had been forbidden;
It taught them nothing new. They hid their pride,
But did not listen much when they were chidden;
They knew exactly what to do outside.

They left: immediately the memory faded
Of all they'd learnt; they could not understand
The dogs now who, before, had always aided;
The stream was dumb with whom they'd always planned.

They wept and quarrelled: freedom was so wild.
In front, maturity, as he ascended,
Retired like a horizon from the child;

The dangers and the punishments grew greater;
And the way back by angels was defended
Against the poet and the legislator.

He turned his field into a meeting-place,
And grew the tolerant ironic eye,
And formed the mobile money-changer's face,
And found the notion of equality.

And strangers were as brothers to his clocks,
And with his spires he made a human sky;
Museums stored his learning like a box,
And paper watched his money like a spy.

It grew so fast his life was overgrown,
And he forgot what once it had been made for,
And gathered into crowds and was alone,

And lived expensively and did without,
And could not find the earth which he had paid for,
Nor feel the love that he knew all about.

XI

GANYMEDE

He looked in all His wisdom from the throne
Down on that humble boy who kept the sheep,
And sent a dove; the dove returned alone:
Youth liked the music, but soon fell asleep.

But He had planned such future for the youth:
Surely, His duty now was to compel.
For later he would come to love the truth,
And own his gratitude. His eagle fell.

It did not work. His conversation bored
The boy who yawned and whistled and made faces,
And wriggled free from fatherly embraces;

But with the eagle he was always willing
To go where it suggested, and adored
And learnt from it so many ways of killing.

XII

A NEW AGE

So an age ended, and its last deliverer died
In bed, grown idle and unhappy; they were safe:
The sudden shadow of a giant's enormous calf
Would fall no more at dusk across their lawns outside.

They slept in peace: in marshes here and there no doubt
A sterile dragon lingered to a natural death,
But in a year the spoor had vanished from the heath:
A kobold's knocking in the mountain petered out.

Only the sculptors and the poets were half sad,
And the pert retinue from the magician's house
Grumbled and went elsewhere. The vanquished powers were
        glad

To be invisible and free; without remorse
Struck down the sons who strayed into their course,
And ravished the daughters, and drove the fathers mad.

XIX

But in the evening the oppression lifted;
The peaks came into focus; it had rained:
Across the lawns and cultured flowers drifted
The conversation of the highly trained.

The gardeners watched them pass and priced their shoes:
A chauffeur waited, reading in the drive,
For them to finish their exchange of views;
It seemed a picture of the private life.

Far off, no matter what good they intended,
The armies waited for a verbal error
With all the instruments for causing pain:

And on the issue of their charm depended
A land laid waste, with all its young men slain,
The women weeping, and the towns in terror.

The life of man is never quite completed;
The daring and the chatter will go on:
But, as an artist feels his power gone,
These walk the earth and know themselves defeated.

Some could not bear nor break the young and mourn for
The wounded myths that once made nations good,
Some lost a world they never understood,
Some saw too clearly all that man was born for.

Loss is their shadow-wife, Anxiety
Receives them like a grand hotel; but where
They may regret they must; their life, to hear

The call of the forbidden cities, see
The stranger watch them with a happy stare,
And Freedom hostile in each home and tree.

One Evening

As I walked out one evening,
    Walking down Bristol Street,
The crowds upon the pavement
    Were fields of harvest wheat.

And down by the brimming river
    I heard a lover sing
Under an arch of the railway:
    'Love has no ending.

'I'll love you, dear, I'll love you
    Till China and Africa meet,
And the river jumps over the mountain
    And the salmon sing in the street.

'I'll love you till the ocean
   Is folded and hung up to dry,
And the seven stars go squawking
   Like geese about the sky.

'The years shall run like rabbits,
   For in my arms I hold
The Flower of the Ages,
   And the first love of the world.'

But all the clocks in the city
   Began to whirr and chime:
'O let not Time deceive you,
   You cannot conquer Time.

'In the burrows of the Nightmare
   Where Justice naked is,
Time watches from the shadow
   And coughs when you would kiss.

'In headaches and in worry
   Vaguely life leaks away,
And Time will have his fancy
   To-morrow or to-day.

'Into many a green valley
   Drifts the appalling snow;
Time breaks the threaded dances
   And the diver's brilliant bow.

'O plunge your hands in water,
   Plunge them in up to the wrist;
Stare, stare in the basin
   And wonder what you've missed.

'The glacier knocks in the cupboard,
   The desert sighs in the bed,
And the crack in the tea-cup opens
   A lane to the land of the dead.

'Where the beggars raffle the banknotes
   And the Giant is enchanting to Jack,
And the Lily-white Boy is a Roarer,
   And Jill goes down on her back.

'O look, look in the mirror,
   O look in your distress;
Life remains a blessing
   Although you cannot bless.

'O stand, stand at the window
   As the tears scald and start;
You shall love your crooked neighbour
   With your crooked heart.'

It was late, late in the evening
   The lovers they were gone;
The clocks had ceased their chiming,
   And the deep river ran on.

Roman Wall Blues

Over the heather the wet wind blows,
I've lice in my tunic and a cold in my nose.

The rain comes pattering out of the sky,
I'm a Wall soldier, I don't know why.

The mist creeps over the hard grey stone,
My girl's in Tungria; I sleep alone.

Aulus goes hanging around her place,
I don't like his manners, I don't like his face.

Piso's a Christian, he worships a fish;
There'd be no kissing if he had his wish.

She gave me a ring but I diced it away;
I want my girl and I want my pay.

When I'm a veteran with only one eye
I shall do nothing but look at the sky.

Epitaph on a Tyrant

Perfection, of a kind, was what he was after,
And the poetry he invented was easy to understand;
He knew human folly like the back of his hand,
And was greatly interested in armies and fleets;
When he laughed, respectable senators burst with laughter,
And when he cried the little children died in the streets.

Three Sonnets from *The Quest*

II

All had been ordered weeks before the start
From the best firms at such work; instruments
To take the measure of all queer events,
And drugs to move the bowels or the heart.

A watch, of course, to watch impatience fly,
Lamps for the dark and shades against the sun;
Foreboding, too, insisted on a gun,
And coloured beads to soothe a savage eye.

In theory they were sound on Expectation
Had there been situations to be in.
Unluckily they were their situation:

One should not give a poisoner medicine,
A conjurer fine apparatus, nor
A rifle to a melancholic bore.

VIII

He watched with all his organs of concern
How princes walk, what wives and children say;
Reopened old graves in his heart to learn
What laws the dead had died to disobey.

And came reluctantly to his conclusion:
'All the arm-chair philosophers are false;
To love another adds to the confusion;
The song of pity is the Devil's Waltz.'

And bowed to fate and was successful so
That soon he was the king of all the creatures:
Yet, shaking in an autumn nightmare, saw,

Approaching down a ruined corridor,
A figure with his own distorted features
That wept, and grew enormous, and cried Woe.

X

They noticed that virginity was needed
To trap the unicorn in every case,

But not that, of those virgins who succeeded,
A high percentage had an ugly face.

The hero was as daring as they thought him,
But his peculiar boyhood missed them all;
The angel of a broken leg had taught him
The right precautions to avoid a fall.

So in presumption they set forth alone
On what, for them, was not compulsory
And stuck half-way to settle in some cave
With desert lions to domesticity;

Or turned aside to be absurdly brave,
And met the ogre and were turned to stone.

Leap Before You Look

The sense of danger must not disappear:
The way is certainly both short and steep,
However gradual it looks from here;
Look, if you like, but you will have to leap.

Tough-minded men get mushy in their sleep
And break the by-laws any fool can keep;
It is not the convention but the fear
That has a tendency to disappear.

The worried efforts of the busy heap,
The dirt, the imprecision, and the beer
Produce a few smart wisecracks every year;
Laugh if you can, but you will have to leap.

The clothes that are considered right to wear
Will not be either sensible or cheap,
So long as we consent to live like sheep
And never mention those who disappear.

Much can be said for social savoir-faire,
But to rejoice when no one else is there
Is even harder than it is to weep;
No one is watching, but you have to leap.

A solitude ten thousand fathoms deep
Sustains the bed on which we lie, my dear:
Although I love you, you will have to leap;
Our dream of safety has to disappear.

A Healthy Spot

They're nice—one would never dream of going over
Any contract of theirs with a magnifying
Glass, or of locking up one's letters—also
Kind and efficient—one gets what one asks for.
Just what is wrong, then, that, living among them,
One is constantly struck by the number of
Happy marriages and unhappy people?
They attend all the lectures on Post-War Problems,
For they do mind, they honestly want to help; yet,
As they notice the earth in their morning papers,
What sense do they make of its folly and horror
Who have never, one is convinced, felt a sudden
Desire to torture the cat or do a strip-tease
In a public place? Have they ever, one wonders,
Wanted so much to see a unicorn, even
A dead one? Probably. But they won't say so,
Ignoring by tacit consent our hunger

For eternal life, that caged rebuked question
Occasionally let out at clambakes or
College reunions, and which the smoke-room story
Alone, ironically enough, stands up for.

If I Could Tell You

Time will say nothing but I told you so,
Time only knows the price we have to pay;
If I could tell you I would let you know.

If we should weep when clowns put on their show,
If we should stumble when musicians play,
Time will say nothing but I told you so.

There are no fortunes to be told, although,
Because I love you more than I can say,
If I could tell you I would let you know.

The winds must come from somewhere when they blow,
There must be reasons why the leaves decay;
Time will say nothing but I told you so.

Perhaps the roses really want to grow,
The vision seriously intends to stay;
If I could tell you I would let you know.

Suppose the lions all get up and go,
And all the brooks and soldiers run away;
Will Time say nothing but I told you so?
If I could tell you I would let you know.

Alonso to Ferdinand

Dear Son, when the warm multitudes cry,
Ascend your throne majestically,
But keep in mind the waters where fish
See sceptres descending with no wish
To touch them; sit regal and erect,
But imagine the sands where a crown
Has the status of a broken-down
Sofa or mutilated statue:
Remember as bells and cannon boom
The cold deep that does not envy you,
The sunburnt superficial kingdom
Where a king is an object.

Expect no help from others, for who
Talk sense to princes or refer to
The scorpion in official speeches
As they unveil some granite Progress
Leading a child and holding a bunch
Of lilies? In their Royal Zoos the
Shark and the octopus are tactfully
Omitted; synchronized clocks march on
Within their powers; without, remain
The ocean flats where no subscription
Concerts are given, the desert plain
Where there is nothing for lunch.

Only your darkness can tell you what
A prince's ornate mirror dare not,
Which you should fear more—the sea in which
A tyrant sinks entangled in rich
Robes while a mistress turns a white back
Upon his splutter, or the desert

Where an emperor stands in his shirt
While his diary is read by sneering
Beggars, and far off he notices
A lean horror flapping and hopping
Toward him with inhuman swiftness:
Learn from your dreams what you lack,

For as your fears are, so must you hope.
The Way of Justice is a tightrope
Where no prince is safe for one instant
Unless he trust his embarrassment,
As in his left ear the siren sings
Meltingly of water and a night
Where all flesh had peace, and on his right
The efreet offers a brilliant void
Where his mind could be perfectly clear
And all his limitations destroyed:
Many young princes soon disappear
To join all the unjust kings.

So, if you prosper, suspect those bright
Mornings when you whistle with a light
Heart. You are loved; you have never seen
The harbour so still, the park so green,
So many well-fed pigeons upon
Cupolas and triumphal arches,
So many stags and slender ladies
Beside the canals. Remember when
Your climate seems a permanent home
For marvellous creatures and great men,
What griefs and convulsions startled Rome,
Ecbatana, Babylon.

How narrow the space, how slight the chance
For civil pattern and importance

Between the watery vagueness and
The triviality of the sand,
How soon the lively trip is over
From loose craving to sharp aversion,
Aimless jelly to paralysed bone;
At the end of each successful day
Remember that the fire and the ice
Are never more than one step away
From the temperate city: it is
But a moment to either.

But should you fail to keep your kingdom
And, like your father before you, come
Where thought accuses and feeling mocks,
Believe your pain; praise the scorching rocks
For their desiccation of your lust,
Thank the bitter treatment of the tide
For its dissolution of your pride,
That the whirlwind may arrange your will
And the deluge release it to find
The spring in the desert, the fruitful
Island in the sea, where flesh and mind
Are delivered from mistrust.

Blue the sky beyond her humming sail
As I sit today by our ship's rail
Watching exuberant porpoises
Escort us homeward and writing this
For you to open when I am gone:
Read it, Ferdinand, with the blessing
Of Alonso, your father, once King
Of Naples, now ready to welcome
Death, but rejoicing in a new love,
A new peace, having heard the solemn
Music strike and seen the statue move
To forgive our illusion.

Miranda's Song

My Dear One is mine as mirrors are lonely,
As the poor and sad are real to the good king,
And the high green hill sits always by the sea.

Up jumped the Black Man behind the elder tree,
Turned a somersault and ran away waving;
My Dear One is mine as mirrors are lonely.

The Witch gave a squawk; her venomous body
Melted into light as water leaves a spring
And the high green hill sits always by the sea.

At his crossroads, too, the Ancient prayed for me;
Down his wasted cheeks tears of joy were running:
My Dear One is mine as mirrors are lonely.

He kissed me awake, and no one was sorry;
The sun shone on sails, eyes, pebbles, anything,
And the high green hill sits always by the sea.

So, to remember our changing garden, we
Are linked as children in a circle dancing:
My Dear One is mine as mirrors are lonely,
And the high green hill sits always by the sea.

from *The Age of Anxiety*

O

Secret meetings at the slaughter-house
With nickels and knives, initiations
Behind the billboards. Then the hammerpond looked
So green and grim, yet graciously its dank

Water made us welcome—once in, we
Swam without swearing. The smelting mill
We broke into had a big chimney
And huge engines; holding our breath, we
Lighted matches and looked at the gears,
The cruel cogwheels, the crank's absolute
Veto on pleasure. In a vacant lot
We built a bonfire and burned alive
Some stolen tyres. How strong and good one
Felt at first, how fagged coming home through
The urban evening. Heavy like us
Sank the gas-tanks—it was supper time.
In hot houses helpless babies and
Telephones gabbled untidy cries,
And on embankments black with burnt grass
Shambling freight-trains were shunted away
Past crimson clouds.

from *The Rake's Progress*

In youth the panting slave pursues
    The fair evasive dame;
Then, caught in colder fetters, woos
    Wealth, office or a name;

Till, old, dishonoured, sick, downcast
    And failing in his wits,
In Virtue's narrow cell at lasts
    The withered bondsman sit.

That man alone his fate fulfills,
    For he alone is free
Who chooses what to will, and wills
    His choice as destiny.

No eye his future can foretell.
  No law his past explain
Whom neither Passion may compel
  Nor Reason can restrain.

Walks

I choose the road from here to there
When I've a scandalous tale to bear,
Tools to return or books to lend
To someone at the other end.

Returning afterwards, although
I meet my footsteps toe to toe,
The road looks altogether new
Now that is done I meant to do.

But I avoid it when I take
A walker's walk for walking's sake:
The repetition it involves
Raises a doubt it never solves.

What good or evil angel bid
Me stop exactly when I did?
What would have happened had I gone
A kilometre further on?

No, when a fidget in the soul
Or cumulous clouds invite a stroll,
The route I pick goes roundabout
To finish where it started out.

It gets me home, this curving track,
Without my having to turn back,
Nor does it leave it up to me
To say how long my walk shall be,

Yet satisfies a moral need
By turning behaviour into deed,
For I have boxed the compass when
I enter my front door again.

The heart, afraid to leave her shell,
Demands a hundred yards as well
Between my personal abode
And either sort of public road,

Making, when it is added too,
The straight a T, the round a Q,
Allowing me in rain or shine
To call both walks entirely mine,

A lane no traveller would use,
Where prints that do not fit my shoes
Have looked for me and, like enough,
Were made by someone whom I love.

Themes and Argument

The Question

To ask the hard question is simple:
Asking at meeting
With the simple glance of acquaintance
To what these go
And how these do;
To ask the hard question is simple,
The simple act of the confused will.

But the answer
Is hard and hard to remember:
On steps or on shore
The ears listening
To words at meeting,
The eyes looking
At the hands helping,
Are never sure
Of what they learn
From how these things are done,

And forgetting to listen or see
Makes forgetting easy,
Only remembering the method of remembering,
Remembering only in another way,
Only the strangely exciting lie,
Afraid
To remember what the fish ignored,
How the bird escaped, or if the sheep obeyed.

Till, losing memory,
Bird, fish, and sheep are ghostly,
And ghosts must do again
What gives them pain.
Cowardice cries
For windy skies,
Coldness for water,
Obedience for a master.

Shall memory restore
The steps and the shore,
The face and the meeting place;
Shall the bird live,
Shall the fish dive,
And sheep obey
In a sheep's way;
Can love remember
The question and the answer,
For love recover
What has been dark and rich and warm all over?

Law Like Love

Law, say the gardeners, is the sun,
Law is the one
All gardeners obey
To-morrow, yesterday, to-day.

Law is the wisdom of the old,
The impotent grandfathers shrilly scold;
The grandchildren put out a treble tongue,
Law is the senses of the young.

Law, says the priest with a priestly look,
Expounding to an unpriestly people,
Law is the words in my priestly book,
Law is my pulpit and my steeple.

Law, says the judge as he looks down his nose,
Speaking clearly and most severely,
Law is as I've told you before,
Law is as you know I suppose,
Law is but let me explain it once more,
Law is The Law.

Yet law-abiding scholars write:
Law is neither wrong nor right,
Law is only crimes
Punished by places and by times,
Law is the clothes men wear
Anytime, anywhere,
Law is Good morning and Good night.

Others say, Law is our Fate;
Others say, Law is our State;
Others say, others say
Law is no more
Law has gone away.

And always the loud angry crowd
Very angry and very loud
Law is We,
And always the soft idiot softly Me.

If we, dear, know we know no more
Than they about the law,
If I no more than you
Know what we should and should not do
Except that all agree
Gladly or miserably

That the law is
And that all know this,
If therefore thinking it absurd
To identify Law with some other word,
Unlike so many men
I cannot say Law is again,
No more than they can we suppress
The universal wish to guess
Or slip out of our own position
Into an unconcerned condition.
Although I can at least confine
Your vanity and mine
To stating timidly
A timid similarity,
We shall boast anyway:
Like love I say.

Like love we don't know where or why
Like love we can't compel or fly
Like love we often weep
Like love we seldom keep.

The Prophets

Perhaps I always knew what they were saying:
Even the early messengers who walked
Into my life from books where they were staying,
Those beautiful machines that never talked

But let the small boy worship them and learn
All their long names whose hardness made him proud;
Love was the word they never said aloud
As something that a picture can't return.

And later when I hunted the Good Place,
Abandoned lead-mines let themselves be caught;
There was no pity in the adit's face,
The rusty winding-engine never taught
One obviously too apt, to say Too Late:
Their lack of shyness was a way of praising
Just what I didn't know, why I was gazing,
While all their lack of answer whispered 'Wait,'
And taught me gradually without coercion,
And all the landscape round them pointed to
The calm with which they took complete desertion
As proof that you existed.

       It was true.
For now I have the answer from the face
That never will go back into a book
But asks for all my life, and is the Place
Where all I touch is moved to an embrace,
And there is no such thing as a vain look.

Another Time

For us like any other fugitive,
Like the numberless flowers that cannot number
And all the beasts that need not remember,
It is to-day in which we live.

So many try to say Not Now,
So many have forgotten how
To say I Am, and would be
Lost, if they could, in history.

Bowing, for instance, with such old-world grace
To a proper flag in a proper place,
Muttering like ancients as they stump upstairs
Of Mine and His or Ours and Theirs.

Just as if time were what they used to will
When it was gifted with possession still,
Just as if they were wrong
In no more wishing to belong.

No wonder then so many die of grief,
So many are so lonely as they die;
No one has yet believed or liked a lie,
Another time has other lives to live.

from *New Year Letter*

(a)   Great masters who have shown mankind
An order it has yet to find,
What if all pedants say of you
As personalities be true?
All the more honour to you then
If, weaker than some other men,
You had the courage that survives
Soiled, shabby, egotistic lives,
If poverty or ugliness
Ill-health or social unsuccess
Hunted you out of life to play
At living in another way;
Yet the live quarry all the same
Were changed to huntsmen in the game,
And the wild furies of the past,
Tracked to their origins at last,
Trapped in a medium's artifice,
To charity, delight, increase.
Now large, magnificent, and calm,
Your changeless presences disarm
The sullen generations, still
The fright and fidget of the will,
And to the growing and the weak
Your final transformations speak;

Saying to dreaming, 'I am deed,'
To striving, 'Courage, I succeed,'
To mourning, 'I remain. Forgive.'
And to becoming, 'I am. Live.'

     .   .   .

(b)   O but it happens every day
To someone. Suddenly the way
Leads straight into their native lands,
The Temenos' small wicket stands
Wide open, shining at the centre
The well of life, and they may enter.
Though compasses and stars cannot
Direct to that magnetic spot,
Nor Will nor willing-not-to-will,
For there is neither good nor ill
But free rejoicing energy,
Yet anytime, how casually,
Out of his organized distress
An accidental happiness,
Catching man off his guard, will blow him
Out of his life in time to show him
The field of Being where he may
Unconscious of Becoming, play
With the Eternal Innocence
In unimpeded utterance.
But perfect Being has ordained
It must be lost to be regained
And in its orchards grows the tree
And fruit of human destiny,
And men must eat it and depart
At once with gay and grateful heart,
Obedient, reborn, re-aware:
For, if he stop an instant there,
The sky grows crimson with a curse,
The flowers change colour for the worse,

He hears behind his back the wicket
Padlock itself, from the dark thicket
The chuckle with no healthy cause,
And helpless, sees the crooked claws
Emerging into view and groping
For handholds on the low round coping,
As Horror clambers from the well:
For he has sprung the trap of Hell.

Hell is the being of the lie
That we become if we deny
The laws of consciousness and claim
Becoming and Being are the same.
Being in time, and man discrete
In will yet free and self-complete;
Its fire the pain to which we go
If we refuse to suffer, though
The one unnecessary grief
Is the vain craving for relief.
When to the suffering we could bear
We add intolerable fear,
Absconding from remembrance, mocked
By our own partial senses, locked
Each in a stale uniqueness, lie
Time-conscious for eternity.

      •   •   •

(c)   More even than in Europe, here
The choice of patterns is made clear
Which the machine imposes, what
Is possible and what is not,
To what conditions we must bow
In building the Just City now.

However we decide to act
Decision must accept the fact

That the machine has now destroyed
The local customs we enjoyed,
Replaced the bonds of blood and nation
By personal confederation:
No longer can we learn our good
From chances of a neighbourhood
Or class or party, or refuse
As individuals to choose
Our loves, authorities, and friends
To judge our means and plan our ends;
For the machine has cried aloud
And publicized among the crowd
The secret that was always true
But known once only to the few,
Compelling all to the admission,
Aloneness is man's real condition,
That each must travel forth alone
In search of the Essential Stone,
The 'Nowhere-without-No' that is
The justice of societies.

from *Prospero to Ariel*

Stay with me, Ariel, while I pack, and with your first free act
    Delight my leaving; share my resigning thoughts
As you have served my revelling wishes: then, brave spirit,
    Ages to you of song and daring, and to me
Briefly Milan, then earth. In all, things have turned out better
    Than I once expected or ever deserved;
I am glad that I did not recover my dukedom till
    I do not want it; I am glad that Miranda
No longer pays me any attention; I am glad I have freed you,
    So at last I can really believe I shall die.
For under your influence death is inconceivable:
    On walks through winter woods, a bird's dry carcass

Agitates the retina with novel images,
     A stranger's quiet collapse in a noisy street
Is the beginning of much lively speculation,
     And every time some dear flesh disappears
What is real is the arriving grief; thanks to your service,
     The lonely and unhappy are very much alive.

But now all these heavy books are no use to me any more, for
     Where I go, words carry no weight: it is best,
Then, I surrender their fascinating counsel
     To the silent dissolution of the sea
Which misuses nothing because it values nothing;
     Whereas man overvalues everything
Yet, when he learns the price is pegged to his valuation,
     Complains bitterly he is being ruined which, of course, he is,
So kings find it odd they should have a million subjects
     Yet share in the thoughts of none, and seducers
Are sincerely puzzled at being unable to love
     What they are able to possess; so, long ago,
In an open boat, I wept at giving a city,
     Common warmth and touching substance, for a gift
In dealing with shadows. If age, which is certainly
     Just as wicked as youth, look any wiser,
It is only that youth is still able to believe
     It will get away with anything, while age
Knows only too well that it has got away with nothing:
     The child runs out to play in the garden, convinced
That the furniture will go on with its thinking lesson,
     Who, fifty years later, if he plays at all,
Will first ask its kind permission to be excused.

     When I woke into my life, a sobbing dwarf
Whom giants served only as they pleased, I was not what I
          seemed;
     Beyond their busy backs I made a magic
To ride away from a father's imperfect justice,

Take vengeance on the Romans for their grammar,
Usurp the popular earth and blot out for ever
    The gross insult of being a mere one among many:
Now, Ariel, I am that I am, your late and lonely master,
    Who knows now what magic is;—the power to enchant
That comes from disillusion. What the books can teach one
    Is that most desires end up in stinking ponds,
But we have only to learn to sit still and give no orders,
    To make you offer us your echo and your mirror;
We have only to believe you, then you dare not lie;
    To ask for nothing, and at once from your calm eyes,
With their lucid proof of apprehension and disorder,
    All we are not stares back at what we are. For all things
In your company, can be themselves: historic deeds
    Drop their hauteur and speak of shabby childhoods
When all they longed for was to join in the gang of doubts
    Who so tormented them; sullen diseases
Forget their dreadful appearance and make silly jokes;
    Thick-headed goodness for once is not a bore.
No one but you had sufficient audacity and eyesight
    To find those clearings where the shy humiliations
Gambol on sunny afternoons, the waterhole to which
    The scarred rogue sorrow comes quietly in the small hours:
And no one but you is reliably informative on hell;
    As you whistle and skip past, the poisonous
Resentments scuttle over your unrevolted feet,
    And even the uncontrollable vertigo,
Because it can scent no shame, is unobliged to strike.

from *For the Time Being*

Well, so that is that. Now we must dismantle the tree,
Putting the decorations back into their cardboard boxes—
Some have got broken—and carrying them up to the attic.

The holly and the mistletoe must be taken down and burnt,
And the children got ready for school. There are enough
Left-overs to do, warmed-up, for the rest of the week—
Not that we have much appetite, having drunk such a lot,
Stayed up so late, attempted—quite unsuccessfully—
To love all of our relatives, and in general
Grossly overestimated our powers. Once again
As in previous years we have seen the actual Vision and failed
To do more than entertain it as an agreeable
Possibility, once again we have sent Him away,
Begging though to remain His disobedient servant,
The promising child who cannot keep His word for long.
The Christmas Feast is already a fading memory,
And already the mind begins to be vaguely aware
Of an unpleasant whiff of apprehension at the thought
Of Lent and Good Friday which cannot, after all, now
Be very far off. But, for the time being, here we all are,
Back in the moderate Aristotelian city
Of darning and the Eight-Fifteen, where Euclid's geometry
And Newton's mechanics would account for our experience,
And the kitchen table exists because I scrub it.
It seems to have shrunk during the holidays. The streets
Are much narrower than we remembered; we had forgotten
The office was as depressing as this. To those who have seen
The Child, however dimly, however incredulously,
The Time Being is, in a sense, the most trying time of all
For the innocent children who whispered so excitedly
Outside the locked door where they knew the presents to be
Grew up when it opened. Now, recollecting that moment
We can repress the joy, but the guilt remains conscious;
Remembering the stable where for once in our lives
Everything became a You and nothing was an It.
And craving the sensation but ignoring the cause,
We look round for something, no matter what, to inhibit
Our self-reflection, and the obvious thing for that purpose
Would be some great suffering. So, once we have met the Son,

We are tempted ever after to pray to the Father;
'Lead us into temptation and evil for our sake.'

They will come, all right, don't worry; probably in a form
That we do not expect, and certainly with a force
More dreadful than we can imagine. In the meantime
There are bills to be paid, machines to keep in repair,
Irregular verbs to learn, the Time Being to redeem
From insignificance. The happy morning is over,
The night of agony still to come; the time is noon:
When the Spirit must practise his scales of rejoicing
God will cheat no one, not even the world of its triumph.

Canzone

When shall we learn, what should be clear as day,
We cannot choose what we are free to love?
Although the mouse we banished yesterday
Is an enraged rhinoceros to-day,
Our value is more threatened than we know:
Shabby objections to our present day
Go snooping round its outskirts; night and day
Faces, orations, battles, bait our will
As questionable forms and noises will;
Whole phyla of resentments every day
Give status to the wild men of the world
Who rule the absent-minded and this world.

We are created from and with the world
To suffer with and from it day by day:
Whether we meet in a majestic world
Of solid measurements or a dream world
Of swans and gold, we are required to love
All homeless objects that require a world.
Our claim to own our bodies and our world
Is our catastrophe. What can we know

But panic and caprice until we know
Our dreadful appetite demands a world
Whose order, origin, and purpose will
Be fluent satisfaction of our will?

Drift, Autumn, drift; fall, colours, where you will:
Bald melancholia minces through the world.
Regret, cold oceans, the lymphatic will
Caught in reflection on the right to will:
While violent dogs excite their dying day
To bacchic fury; snarl, though, as they will,
Their teeth are not a triumph for the will
But utter hesitation. What we love
Ourselves for is our power not to love,
To shrink to nothing or explode at will,
To ruin and remember that we know
What ruins and hyaenas cannot know.

If in this dark now I less often know
That spiral staircase where the haunted will
Hunts for its stolen luggage, who should know
Better than you, beloved, how I know
What gives security to any world,
Or in whose mirror I begin to know
The chaos of the heart as merchants know
Their coins and cities, genius its own day?
For through our lively traffic all the day,
In my own person I am forced to know
How much must be forgotten out of love,
How much must be forgiven, even love.

Dear flesh, dear mind, dear spirit, O dear love,
In the depths of myself blind monsters know
Your presence and are angry, dreading Love
That asks its images for more than love;
The hot rampageous horses of my will,

Catching the scent of Heaven, whinny: Love
Gives no excuse to evil done for love,
Neither in you, nor me, nor armies, nor the world
Of words and wheels, nor any other world.
Dear fellow-creature, praise our God of Love
That we are so admonished, that no day
Of conscious trial be a wasted day.

Or else we make a scarecrow of the day,
Loose ends and jumble of our common world,
And stuff and nonsense of our own free will;
Or else our changing flesh may never know
There must be sorrow if there can be love.

from *The Age of Anxiety*

For the others, like me, there is only the flash
Of negative knowledge, the night when, drunk, one
Staggers to the bathroom and stares in the glass
To meet one's madness, when what mother said seems
Such darling rubbish and the decent advice
Of the liberal weeklies as lost an art
As peasant pottery, for plainly it is not
To the Cross or to Clarté or to Common Sense
Our passions pray but to primitive totems
As absurd as they are savage; science or no science,
It is Bacchus or the Great Boyg or Baal-Peor,
Fortune's Ferris-wheel or the physical sound
Of our own names which they actually adore as their
Ground and goal. Yet the grossest of our dreams is
No worse than our worship which for the most part
Is so much galimatias to get out of
Knowing our neighbour, all the needs and conceits of
The poor muddled maddened mundane animal
Who is hostess to us all, for each contributes his

Personal panic, his predatory note
To her gregarious grunt as she gropes in the dark
For her lost lollypop. We belong to our kind,
Are judged as we judge, for all gestures of time
And all species of space respond in our own
Contradictory dialect, the double talk
Of ambiguous bodies, born like us to that
Natural neighbourhood which denial itself
Like a friend confirms; they reflect our status,
Temporals pleading for external life with
The infinite impetus of anxious spirits,
Finite in fact yet refusing to be real,
Wanting our own way, unwilling to say Yes
To the Self-So which is the same at all times,
That Always-Opposite which is the whole subject
Of our not-knowing, yet from no necessity
Condescended to exist and to suffer death
And, scorned on a scaffold, ensconced in His life
The human household. In our anguish we struggle
To elude Him, to lie to Him, yet His love observes
His appalling promise; His predilection
As we wander and weep is with us to the end,
Minding our meanings, our least matter dear to Him,
His Good ingressant on our gross occasions
Envisages our advance, valuing for us
Though our bodies too blind or too bored to examine
What sorts excite them are slain interjecting
Their childish Ows and, in choosing how many
And how much they will love, our minds insist on
Their own disorder as their own punishment,
His Question disqualifies our quick senses,
His Truth makes our theories historical sins,
It is where we are wounded that is when He speaks
Our creaturely cry, concluding His children
In their mad unbelief to have mercy on them all
As they wait unawares for His World to come.

Their Lonely Betters

As I listened from a beach-chair in the shade
To all the noises that my garden made,
It seemed to me only proper that words
Should be withheld from vegetables and birds.

A robin with no Christian name ran through
The Robin-Anthem which was all it knew,
And rustling flowers for some third party waited
To say which pairs, if any, should get mated.

Not one of them was capable of lying,
There was not one which knew that it was dying
Or could have with a rhythm or a rhyme
Assumed responsibility for time.

Let them leave language to their lonely betters
Who count some days and long for certain letters;
We, too, make noises when we laugh or weep,
Words are for those with promises to keep.

Memorial for the City

In the self-same point that our soul is made sensual, in the self-same point is the City of God ordained to him from without beginning.

JULIANA OF NORWICH

The eyes of the crow and the eye of the camera open
Onto Homer's world, not ours. First and last
They magnify earth, the abiding
Mother of gods and men; if they notice either

It is only in passing: gods behave, men die,
Both feel in their own small way, but She
Does nothing and does not care,
She alone is seriously there.

The crow on the crematorium chimney
And the camera roving the battle
Record a space where time has no place.
On the right a village is burning, in a market-town to the left
The soldiers fire, the mayor bursts into tears,
The captives are led away, while far in the distance
A tanker sinks into a dedolant sea.
That is the way things happen; for ever and ever
Plum-blossom falls on the dead, the roar of the waterfall
    covers
The cries of the whipped and the sighs of the lovers
And the hard bright light composes
A meaningless moment into an eternal fact
Which a whistling messenger disappears with into a defile:
One enjoys glory, one endures shame;
He may, she must. There is no one to blame.
The steady eyes of the crow and the camera's candid eye
See as honestly as they know how, but they lie.
The crime of life is not time. Even now, in this night
Among the ruins of the Post-Vergilian City
Where our past is a chaos of graves and the barbed-wire
    stretches ahead
Into our future till it is lost to sight,
Our grief is not Greek: As we bury our dead
We know without knowing there is reason for what we bear,
That our hurt is a desertion, that we are to pity
Neither ourselves nor our city;
Whoever the searchlights catch, whatever the loudspeakers
    blare,
We are not to despair.

Precious Five

Be patient, solemn nose,
Serve in a world of prose
The present moment well
Nor surlily contrast
Its brash ill-mannered smell
With grand scents of the past;
That calm enchanted wood,
That grave world where you stood
So gravely at its middle,
Its oracle and riddle,
Has all been altered, now
In anxious times you serve
As bridge from mouth to brow,
An asymmetric curve
Thrust outward from a face
Time-conscious into space,
Whose oddness may provoke
To a mind-saving joke
A mind that would it were
An apathetic sphere:
Point, then, for honour's sake
Up the storm-beaten slope
From memory to hope
The way you cannot take.

Be modest, lively ears,
Spoiled darlings of a stage
Where any caper cheers
The paranoic mind
Of this undisciplined
And concert-going age,
So lacking in conviction
It cannot take pure fiction

And what it wants from you
Are rumours partly true;
Before you catch its sickness
Submit your lucky quickness

And levity to rule,
Go back again to school,
Drudge patiently until
No whisper is too much
And your precision such
At any sound that all
Seem natural, not one
Fantastic or banal,
And then do what you will:
Dance with angelic grace,
In ecstasy and fun,
The luck you cannot place.

Be civil, hands; on you
Although you cannot read
Is written what you do
And blows you struck so blindly
In temper or in greed,
Your tricks of long ago,
Eyes, kindly or unkindly,
Unknown to you will know;
Revere those hairy wrists
And leg-of-mutton fists
Which pulverized the trolls
And carved deep Donts in stone,
Great hands which under knolls
Are now disjointed bone,
But what has been has been;
A tight arthritic claw
Or aldermanic paw
Waving about in praise

Of those homeric days
Is impious and obscene
Grow, hands, into those living
Hands which true hands should be
By making and by giving
To hands you cannot see.

Look, naked eyes, look straight
At all eyes but your own
Lest in a tête-à-tête
Of glances double-crossed,
Both knowing and both known,
Your nakedness be lost;
Rove curiously about
But look from inside out,
Compare two eyes you meet
By dozens on the street,
One shameless, one ashamed,
Too lifeless to be blamed,
With eyes met now and then
Looking from living men,
Which in petrarchan fashion
Play opposite the heart,
Their humour to her passion,
Her nature to their art,
For mutual undeceiving;
True seeing is believing
(What sight can never prove)
There is a world to see:
Look outward, eyes, and love
Those eyes you cannot be.

Praise, tongue, the Earthly Muse
By number and by name
In any style you choose,
For nimble tongues and lame

Have both found favour; praise
Her port and sudden ways,
Now fish-wife and now queen,
Her reason and unreason:
Though freed from that machine,
Praise Her revolving wheel
Of appetite and season
In honour of Another,
The old self you become

At any drink or meal,
That animal of taste
And of his twin, your brother,
Unlettered, savage, dumb,
Down there below the waist:
Although your style be fumbling,
Half stutter and half song,
Give thanks however bumbling,
Telling of Her dear sake
To whom all styles belong
The truth She cannot make.

Be happy, precious five,
So long as I'm alive
Nor try to ask me what
You should be happy for;
Think, if it helps, of love
Or alcohol or gold,
But do as you are told.
I could (which you cannot)
Find reasons fast enough
To face the sky and roar
In anger and despair
At what is going on,
Demanding that it name
Whoever is to blame:

The sky would only wait
Till all my breath was gone
And then reiterate
As if I wasn't there
That singular command
I do not understand,
Bless what there is for being,
Which has to be obeyed, for
What else am I made for,
Agreeing or disagreeing.

The Shield of Achilles

She looked over his shoulder
   For vines and olive trees,
Marble well-governed cities
   And ships upon untamed seas,
But there on the shining metal
   His hands had put instead
An artificial wilderness
   And a sky like lead.

A plain without a feature, bare and brown,
   No blade of grass, no sign of neighbourhood,
Nothing to eat and nowhere to sit down,
   Yet, congregated on its blankness, stood
   An unintelligible multitude.
A million eyes, a million boots in line,
Without expression, waiting for a sign.

Out of the air a voice without a face
   Proved by statistics that some cause was just

In tones as dry and level as the place:
    No one was cheered and nothing was discussed;
    Column by column in a cloud of dust
They marched away enduring a belief
Whose logic brought them, somewhere else, to grief.

        She looked over his shoulder
            For ritual pieties,
        White flower-garlanded heifers,
            Libation and sacrifice,
        But there on the shining metal
            Where the altar should have been,
        She saw by his flickering forge-light
            Quite another scene.

Barbed wire enclosed an arbitrary spot
    Where bored officials lounged (one cracked a joke)
And sentries sweated for the day was hot:
    A crowd of ordinary decent folk
    Watched from without and neither moved nor spoke
As three pale figures were led forth and bound
To three posts driven upright in the ground.

The mass and majesty of this world, all
    That carries weight and always weighs the same
Lay in the hands of others; they were small
    And could not hope for help and no help came:
    What their foes liked to do was done, their shame
Was all the worst could wish; they lost their pride
And died as men before their bodies died.

        She looked over his shoulder
            For athletes at their games,
        Men and women in a dance
            Moving their sweet limbs

Quick, quick, to music,
But there on the shining shield
His hands had set no dancing-floor
But a weed-choked field.

A ragged urchin, aimless and alone,
Loitered about that vacancy, a bird
Flew up to safety from his well-aimed stone:
That girls are raped, that two boys knife a third,
Were axioms to him, who'd never heard
Of any world where promises were kept,
Or one could weep because another wept.

The thin-lipped armourer,
Hephaestos hobbled away,
Thetis of the shining breasts
Cried out in dismay
At what the god had wrought
To please her son, the strong
Iron-hearted man-slaying Achilles
Who would not live long.

Prime

Simultaneously, as soundlessly,
Spontaneously, suddenly
As, at the vaunt of the dawn, the kind
Gates of the body fly open
To its world beyond, the gates of the mind,
The horn gate and the ivory gate
Swing to, swing shut, instantaneously
Quell the nocturnal rummage
Of its rebellious fronde, ill-favoured,
Ill-natured and second-rate,

Disenfranchised, widowed and orphaned
　　By an historical mistake:
Recalled from the shades to be a seeing being,
　　From absence to be on display,
Without a name of history I wake
　　Between my body and the day.

Holy this moment, wholly in the right,
　　As, in complete obedience
To the light's laconic outcry, next
　　As a sheet, near as a wall,
Out there as a mountain's poise of stone,
　　The world is present, about,
And I know that I am, here, not alone
　　But with a world and rejoice
Unvexed, for the will has still to claim
　　This adjacent arm as my own,
The memory to name me, resume
　　Its routine of praise and blame
And smiling to me is this instant while
　　Still the day is intact, and I
The Adam sinless in our beginning,
　　Adam still previous to any act.

I draw breath; this is of course to wish
　　No matter what, to be wise,
To be different, to die and the cost,
　　No matter how, is Paradise
Lost of course and myself owing a death:
　　The eager ridge, the steady sea,
The flat roofs of the fishing village
　　Still asleep in its bunny,
Though as fresh and sunny still are not friends
　　But things to hand, this ready flesh
No honest equal, but my accomplice now
　　My assassin to be, and my name

Stands for my historical share of care
    For a lying self-made city,
Afraid of our living task, the dying
    Which the coming day will ask.

Objects

All that which lies outside our sort of why,
Those wordless creatures who are there as well,
Remote from mourning yet in sight and cry,
Make time more golden than we meant to tell.

Tearless, their surfaces appear as deep
As any longing we believe we had;
If shapes can so to their own edges keep,
No separation proves a being bad.

There is less grief than wonder on the whole,
Even at sunset, though of course we care
Each time the same old shadow falls across

One Person who is not: somewhere, a soul,
Light in her bestial substance, well aware,
Extols the silence of how soon a loss.

Friday's Child

*(In memory of Dietrich Bonhoeffer, martyred
at Flossenburg, April 9th, 1945)*

He told us we were free to choose
    But, children as we were, we thought—
'Paternal Love will only use
    Force in the last resort

On those too bumptious to repent.'—
Accustomed to religious dread,
It never crossed our minds He meant
    Exactly what He said.

Perhaps He frowns, perhaps He grieves,
But it seems idle to discuss
If anger or compassion leaves
    The bigger bangs to us.

What reverence is rightly paid
To a Divinity so odd
He lets the Adam whom He made
    Perform the Acts of God?

It might be jolly if we felt
Awe at this Universal Man;
(When kings were local, people knelt)
    Some try to, but who can?

The self-observed observing Mind
We meet when we observe at all
Is not alarming or unkind
    But utterly banal.

Though instruments at Its command
Make wish and counterwish come true,
It clearly cannot understand
    What It can clearly do.

Since the analogies are rot
Our senses based belief upon,
We have no means of learning what
    Is really going on,

And must put up with having learned
All proofs or disproofs that we tender
Of His existence are returned
    Unopened to the sender.

Now, did He really break the seal
And rise again? We dare not say;
But conscious unbelievers feel
    Quite sure of Judgment Day.

Meanwhile, a silence on the cross,
As dead as we shall ever be,
Speaks of some total gain or loss,
    And you and I are free

To guess from the insulted face
Just what Appearances He saves
By suffering in a public place
    A death reserved for slaves.

Notes

All the books listed here are published by Faber & Faber Ltd., with the exception of THE RAKE'S PROGRESS, which is published by Boosey & Hawkes Ltd.

Each note names the volume in which the poem first appeared. To save space, these abbreviations are used:

POEMS (1930), which includes	P. 1930
Paid on Both Sides, a Charade in verse	P.B.S.
THE ORATORS (1932), an English Study, verse and prose	OR.
THE DOG BENEATH THE SKIN (1935), Drama in verse and prose, with Christopher Isherwood	DOG
LOOK, STRANGER! (1936), Poems	L.S.
LETTERS FROM ICELAND (1937), Travel-Book, verse and prose, with Louis MacNeice	L.I.
JOURNEY TO A WAR (1939), Travel-Book, with Christopher Isherwood; includes	J.W.
In Time of War, a sonnet-sequence with a verse commentary	I.T.W.
ANOTHER TIME (1940), Verse	A.T.
NEW YEAR LETTER (1941), Verse, includes long title-poem, a prologue and epilogue and a sonnet-sequence, *The Quest*	N.Y.L.
FOR THE TIME BEING (1945), a Christmas Oratorio, Verse; contains also	F.T.B.
The Sea and the Mirror, a Commentary, mainly in verse, on Shakespeare's *The Tempest*	S.M.

THE AGE OF ANXIETY (1948), a Baroque Eclogue, Verse   A.A.

COLLECTED SHORTER POEMS, 1930–44 (1950)   C.S.P.

THE RAKE'S PROGRESS (1951), an Opera, music by I.   R.P.
Stravinsky, libretto by Auden and Kallman

NONES (1952), Verse   N.

THE SHIELD OF ACHILLES (1955), Verse   S.A.

HOMAGE TO CLIO (1960), Verse   H.C.

Section One

THE LETTER (P. 1930. V. p. 47)
The Wanderer comes down from a bare upland to the valley,
to be involved again with personal relationships.

THE WATERSHED (P. 1930. XI. p. 56)
The landscape of disused industrialism, decayed and haunting,
which Auden likes. And the favoured figure of the lonely individual who makes an effort, hopefully. The poem uses selected
detail in a way Auden developed further, later in the decade.

MISSING (P. 1930. XXIV. p. 78)
Short-lined early poem, of upland landscape and leaders. The
leaders have separated themselves from the crowd and seek
positive improvement.
It has the melodramatic note of menace and threat which occurs
in many Thirties poems.

TALLER TO-DAY (P. 1930. XXVI. p. 82)
This poem has all the usual properties of the Journey: challenge,
wandering and action—and suggests its emotional attractions
and nostalgia.

Adversary: presumably Death, or the Death Wish

glacier: with Auden, a common symbol for a condition of
frozen inability to act

THE JOURNEY (P. 1930. P.B.S. p. 28 Chorus)
A simple form of the Wanderer theme and of the call to set out.
There is the usual hope, energy and rejection of 'the old life'
which has gone dead.

CHORUS (P. 1930. II. p. 43)
There is a debt to the Middle English West Midland homily,
'Sawles Warde', which dates probably from the early thirteenth
century. There is also much in common with an Old English
poem 'The Wanderer'. The Old English or Anglo-Saxon influence can be easily seen in the alliteration, the line-breaks and
the 'kenning' (poetical paraphrasing: 'houses for fishes' = sea).
We find Auden's usual early ellipsis, with omission of articles
and connectives, and in the last verse a typical Auden simile.
Again, a mood of menace, with the Wanderer bent on positive
action, alone but nostalgic for home.

doom: judgement or Fate

tiger: seems to jar, since it suggests colour and the East—neither
in place in so grey a poem

A SUMMER NIGHT 1933 (L.S. II. p. 13)
The warmth of friendships, overshadowed by political events
and by the responsibilities which flow from them.
Mr Alvarez fairly describes the poem as 'excellent in [its] inventive, easy-going, allusive way'. Is it too easy-going in parts?
See the epithets, similes, personification, social and psychological
details.
In the version printed later in C.S.P. several verses are cut. The
two versions are worth comparing, so as to consider the possible reasons for making these cuts.

PAYSAGE MORALISÉ (L.S. VII. p. 22)
A moralized—allegorical or symbolic—landscape. Wandering,
leaving home, the need for action and hope: the usual symbols.
The form of the poem is that called a *sestina*.

THROUGH THE LOOKING GLASS (L.S. IX. p. 25)

Moving nostalgia for home and family; uncertainty about where to go and what to do (it is unusual to find a poem by Auden so uncertain or, indeed, about uncertainty). He seems to be reminding himself that one need not push at life too insistently.

There are some fine effects. The memories of childhood have an attractive Alice in Wonderland quality.

THE WATCHERS (L.S. X. p. 28)

The rules of order and limit ('O Lords of Limit') are invoked—to control and reduce neurotic extremes.

Helensburg: a small town in Dunbarton, Scotland. Auden was teaching there

JOURNEY TO ICELAND (L.I. p. 25)

The journey to the island seen as a sort of escape; yet there can be no escape from our problems; Iceland is as much involved in them as anywhere else; we must go on, positively, facing problems.

A poem called 'Islands' in the later group of 'Bucolics' is worth comparing.

The final verse has a typical rhetorical gesture. Some of these last lines were frugally saved from an earlier sonnet (not now included in Auden's collected works), 'The fruit in which your parents hid you, boy'.

ports: was originally 'poets' in Auden's typescript. A printer's error made it 'ports' and Auden kept it, since it seemed more evocative than the original

glacier: see earlier note

The alterations made to the original poem are complex and interesting (see L.I.)

THE DEAD ECHO (L.I. p. 227)

From the 'Letter to William Coldstream, Esq.' (an artist), a lyrical dialogue between various lovers of life and Death, acting as Chorus. Death asserts that life is no more than a formal dance; the maggot of decay is everywhere.

Narcissus: a Greek youth who fell in love with his own reflection and died as a result. Hence, destroying self-love

NEW YEAR LETTER (lines 1096–1152. pp. 54–6)
The landscape is that of the typical Northern Pennines, partly bare and partly industrialized though decayed. This is a simple instance of Auden's landscape as symbol.

The poem begins with man's original wildness and moves on to his 'faulting into consciousness', his elemental urge to 'civilize and to create', to understand himself.

'In Praise of Limestone', a few pages further on, is worth comparing.

Urmutterfurcht: a feeling of attraction combined with fear towards the original (Ur) Mother. So, partly, the wish for the womb and for oblivion. The word is from Wagner's (1813–1883) opera *Siegfried* in The Ring Cycle

Das Weibliche: The Feminine Principle. The word is from Goethe's *Faust* (1832)

'*O deine Mutter . . . mein Bild.*'—'Thy mother does not return to thee. I am thyself, thy Duty and Love. They [the ripples on a stream] destroyed my reflection.' Siegfried, who is speaking, is drawn to immerse himself (lose himself) in the stream—as Auden is obscurely drawn to the mine-mouth ('the reservoir of darkness stirred'). Again from Wagner's *Siegfried*. The general sense of all the above is, therefore, the urge to go back to some deep, elemental Earth (Mother) centre

adit: a horizontal entry to a mine

ATLANTIS (C.S.P. p. 37)
The Wanderer again, this time on a symbolic journey, an inner Quest for Truth. The poem runs over various deceptions and insists on the need to recognize them; the journey can never be ended.

In contrast with the theme, the tone is light. This is an instance of the light-toned yet serious verse described in the Introduction.

Atlantis: a mythical island of perfect harmony

Ionia: its school of philosophy formed the starting-point of all Greek philosophy

Thrace: on the north coast of the Aegean, home of Dionysus (and of Orpheus) and so associated with dance and song

conch: a shell used as an instrument

Carthage and Corinth: both in ancient times reputed to be immoral cities

'Give thanks and lie down in peace': see Simeon in Luke 2:25

Hermes: the Greek Mercury

Kabiri: presumably Kabeiroi, an ancient Mediterranean religious cult

THE AGE OF ANXIETY

An example of the Anglo-Saxon line may be useful (this is from *Anglo-Saxon Poetry*, selected and translated by Prof. R. K. Gordon. Everyman ed.)

Wérodes	wísa	wórd-hord	onleac
Of the troop	*the leader*	*word-hoard*	*unlocked*

Note alliteration, half-lines, 'kenning' (periphrasis, as in the second half-line)

(a) from the Prologue. pp. 27-8

The Prologue is ending. A group of lonely people have met in a New York bar. Malin, one of them, is speaking. He invites them to consider together man's life in time. His theme is, once more, the Quest—self-consciousness, anxiety, incompleteness

(b) from Part III. The Seven Stages. pp. 65-6

The youngest of the group, Emble, is speaking, as they begin the Second Stage. Again, it is a Quest and an exile. He sees it as a search for a girl, though it has a deeper meaning; it points to a feeling all can have, that we do not belong, have lost touch with some greater thing (i.e. God)

The detail has some witty, cinematically visual, touches

IN PRAISE OF LIMESTONE (N. p. 11)

The lines are not counted in feet but syllabically. They have alternately thirteen and eleven syllables. There is elision of all contiguous vowels as well as through 'h'. It is worth examining how far this line, and the interwoven alliteration, contribute to the effect Auden wants. A fuller description of this poem is in the Introduction.

The landscape is probably the Italian Apennines. It obviously has much in common with that of the Northern Pennines.

gennels: probably a North Country dialect word for a narrow way between buildings

slamming the door: Goebbels, the Nazi leader, said: 'If we are defeated, we shall slam the door of history behind us'

PLAINS (S.A. 'Bucolics.' p. 27)

One of the later 'Bucolics', poems of symbolic landscape. A psychological and historical reflection on the horror of un-defined space or openness, our fear of losing our sense of identity. The comically off-beat tone is fairly typical. Auden, we re-member, dislikes the notion of 'decorum' in poetry.

Ovid's charmer: it is difficult to find a particular passage in Ovid with which to associate this allusion. Cupid may be meant

genera: plural of 'genus' (species)

Clio: the muse of historical poetry

Tarquin: he raped Lucrece

Section Two

CHORUS FROM P.B.S. (P. 1930. p. 21)

Thirties industrial landscape; man's psychological distress; the need for hopeful action. The selected detailing, so common in the Thirties, is already apparent.

The off-rhymes or near-rhymes ('killed/Cold') are probably a debt to Wilfred Owen, a poet of the First World War.

THE QUESTIONER WHO SITS SO SLY (P. 1930. I. p. 41)

Early, short-lined, elliptical, this has some of the epigrammatic phrases which are so easily remembered ('Stork-legged heaven-reachers').

The theme is again the need for positive choice and action against the temptations to failing will—to all that makes for death.

A FREE ONE (P. 1930. IV. p. 46)

A psychological cameo, with the eye on telling gestures. The subject is a 'public' face which hides inner uncertainties. The rhymes here fall on the unaccented syllables.

SHUT YOUR EYES AND OPEN YOUR MOUTH (P. 1930. XIV. p. 59)

Another elliptical and gnomic poem, again about the way a face, though suggesting strength, may really indicate fundamental weakness. The usual telling detail.

This poem (even more than some other early ones) seems to have been influenced by Laura Riding's poetry. See *A Joking Word* (Cape 1930).

This poem has been described as 'elaborately coy'. Do you agree?

1929: SECTION IV (P. 1930. XVI. p. 65)

Social and psychological observation, decay and threat, in the Thirties. The death of old habits, not only social but personal, is needed.

Some interesting grotesque or surrealist touches. A few lines from the end there is some nicely pointed epigrammatic writing, but the last two lines are vague.

CONSIDER (P. 1930. XXIX. p. 87)
Typical Thirties mood and landscape. Notice the Hawk and Airman. The socio-psychological comment produces some memorable phrases, but some are 'knowing'.

supreme Antagonist: presumably Death

PETITION (P. 1930. XXX. p. 89)
An address to an unnamed 'Sir' (this was written before Auden became a Christian).
One of the best known of the Thirties poems—brilliant in parts. The ending recalls self-conscious documentary films from the Thirties.

THE DOG BENEATH THE SKIN (Opening Chorus p. 11)
Few poems have so many of Auden's predominant Thirties manners: the wide-ranging eye, moving panoramically like a film camera; the perceptive detail; economic and political geography; the portentously cosmic touch at the end, and the drum-beating for moral reform. The observation has that 'external' quality discussed in the Introduction.
Auden seems now to have rejected this poem, which is a pity.

Blue Bird: a car which held the world's land speed record in the Thirties

Bristol Bomber: at the time, an advanced aircraft

THE WITNESSES (DOG. p. 15)
In *The Dog Beneath the Skin* this is sung by Both Leaders. The poem was originally part of a longer poem (1933) with the above title. It creates the sense of menace—partly, one guesses, for the fun of writing an incantatory 'bogeyman' poem.
Some of the figures are from folklore and fairy-tale, perhaps

especially from the German story, *Struwwelpeter* (H. Hoffman, 1847). 'The expansive moments of constricted lives' is typical of one kind of clinical, definite article, selection.

This poem seems also to have been rejected.

The Witnesses: probably the two witnesses of the Apocalypse (Rev. XI, 3–10)

PERHAPS (L.S. I. Prologue p. 11)
Human geography; Thirties observation; landscape. The epigram in verse 10 is neat but cold. 'Love' appears again, in its undefined Thirties form.

Pillars: probably the Pillars of Hercules, the opposing rocks at the exit from the Mediterranean into the Atlantic (that is, Gibraltar and Mount Hacho)

OUR HUNTING FATHERS (L.S. III. p. 17)
Political decisions and moral choices today (compared with those made by our ancestors). The way the epithets work and the modulation of tone between the two stanzas are worth attention. The poem can be compared with W. B. Yeats's 'Death' and Michael Roberts's 'The Images of Death'.

'*To hunger . . .*': from a letter by the Russian Revolutionary leader, Lenin

WHO'S WHO (L.S. XIII. p. 33)
A psychological cameo in sonnet form. It is clever but cute; the structure, and changes of tone, increase the effect of cuteness.

THE MALVERNS (L.S. XVII. p. 42)
The Hawk and the Landscape; some shrewd socio-economic observation; some rhetoric of menace; some clinical 'type-casting' of 'ordinary' people; and some warmth.

This poem has been much altered. A comparison with the original in L.S. is interesting.

Wilfred: the poet Wilfred Owen

Kathy: the short-story writer Katherine Mansfield

antre: cave or cavern

A BRIDE IN THE THIRTIES (L.S. XXI. p. 50)

Home, personal and psychological problems, society and politics. Verse 8 seems to use film technique, again—to present a middle-class childhood as in a series of film-shots.

Van der Lubbe: a young man accused by the Nazis of burning the Reichstag (the German Parliament building) in the Thirties. British left-wing opinion then believed he had been made a scapegoat by the Nazis, who had burned the building themselves. Recent evidence suggests that Van der Lubbe did in fact start the fire

BIRTHDAY POEM (L.S. XXX. p. 63)

There is some very effective Thirties reportage, especially in the first verse. The early and undefined 'Love' appears again. A comparison with Louis MacNeice's *Eclogue for Christmas* is worth making.

Tennyson's island: the Isle of Wight

stoves and resignations: this line recalls a typical mood in the plays of the Russian author Chekhov (1860–1904). His characters were often members of the decaying upper classes condemned to sitting round their living-room stoves on their estates, far from Moscow

fed it with the Jews: a reference to anti-semitic outrages

MACAO (J.W. p. 22)

A sonnet on human geography, shrewdly observed.

Macao: a Portuguese colony on an island off the south coast of China

'HERE WAR IS SIMPLE . . .' (I.T.W. XVI. J.W. p. 274)

A sonnet written on visiting the Sino-Japanese war. He attempts, quietly, as if he were recording with a camera, to capture the misery of the situation in a series of successive visual images.

Dachau: a German concentration camp for Jews and political opponents

FROM 'THE COMMENTARY' (I.T.W. J.W. p. 299)
This excerpt forms the end of 'The Commentary'.

slanting radiations: i.e. the cities of Western Europe

MUSÉE DES BEAUX ARTS (A.T. I. XXI. p. 47)
Set in Brussels. Auden looks at many pictures, but especially at the 'Icarus'. Icarus, in Greek legend, flew too near the sun with wax wings and fell when they melted. (So, a symbol of human aspiration)
A typically understated conversational poem, very competently managed. In some respects, too easily managed. One notices especially the camera eye, searching for the significant visual 'shot'. Such a moment excites Auden's dramatic imagination.
His predominant interest in 'the *human* condition' comes out well from a comparison with Stephen Spender's *The Sad Standards.*

THE COMPOSER (A.T. I. XXII. p. 48)
A cameo about a type (cf. 'The Novelist') in sonnet form. There is a nice ambiguity in 'pure contraption' and 'absolute gift', between the colloquial and the more proper meanings.

MATTHEW ARNOLD (A.T. I. XXVII. p. 58)
Auden is using a common interpretation of Matthew Arnold's career (he stopped writing poetry at a comparatively early age): that it was overshadowed by the influence of his father, Thomas Arnold, Headmaster of Rugby School. The poem puts Arnold's career into a nutshell, very cleverly and pithily ('And thrust his gift . . .'). But, as so often, it seems in parts slick.

THE UNKNOWN CITIZEN (A.T. II. VII. p. 96)
Witty, low-pressure, conversational verse on the centralization and mechanization of human life.

scab: a worker who will not fulfil his Trade Union obligations

SPAIN, 1937 (A.T. Pt. III. No. I. p. 103)

The most celebrated of all Thirties poems, it originally sold as a pamphlet at a shilling; the author's royalties went to 'Medical Aid for Spain'. It contains many examples of the best and the worst of Auden's most typical writing at this time.

A comparison with Stephen Spender's *Vienna* brings out Auden's greater objectivity and selective power, and Spender's greater personal sensitivity.

cromlech: prehistoric stone structure

furious Papa: God as a Freudian father figure

IN MEMORY OF W. B. YEATS (A.T. Pt. III. No. II. p. 107)

See the Introduction for some reference to Auden's deep admiration for Yeats and, in particular, for Yeats's conversational verse.

The changes of tone between the sections are worth examining.

Bourse: foreign stock-exchange (usually Paris)

parish of rich women: a reference to such women as Lady Gregory, with whom Yeats had a close and long-standing relationship

1ST SEPTEMBER 1939 (A.T. Pt. III. No. IV. p. 113)

The most impressive summing-up of the decade in verse. The line is drawn from W. B. Yeats and is worth comparing, in its command, with that in Yeats's *Easter 1916*.

Some amendments are interesting. This is the later version from C.S.P.

1st Sept. 1939: the day the Germans attacked Poland and so started the Second World War

52nd Street: in New York City

Luther: German theologian and founder of Protestantism

Linz: Adolf Hitler went to school there

Thucydides: Athenian historian

neutral air: at this time America had not entered the war

Nijinsky: Russian ballet dancer

Diaghilev: Director of the Russian ballet in the early years of this century

commuters: daily travellers to work

Eros: human love and desire (used in Freudian psychology)

Section Three

WHAT'S IN YOUR MIND . . . (P. 1930. XIII. p. 58)
A lyric and satiric address to a loved one.

THIS LUNAR BEAUTY (P. 1930. XVII. p. 67)
A short-lined early poem, again showing the influence of Laura Riding and Robert Graves. Auden likes incantatory chants—here the effect is to suggest the strange, lunar beauty of the title.

THIS ONE (P. 1930. XVIII. p. 68)
Technically similar to the poem above. Another incantatory poem, this time on the necessary break with 'the old gang' (though there is loss and nostalgia in the process).

THE DECOYS (OR. p. 67)
The poem works entirely through symbols—suggesting how we may destroy the most tender and valuable elements in ourselves, *by* ourselves.

THE SONG OF THE FIRST MAD LADY (DOG. p. 65)
This poem has been included because, using some of the tricks of popular song, it suggests a touching loss most evocatively. Parts have been taken from an earlier sonnet, now discarded.

THE TWO CHORUS LEADERS. (DOG. p. 115)
A typical celebration of stillness in the community of love.

succubus: a demon in female form

SEASCAPE (L.S. V. p. 19)
One of the best known of all Auden's lyrics; a virtuoso piece

(see the vowel-play and the way the line is made to act out the movement of the gull's flight).

AUTUMN SONG (L.S. VIII. p. 24)
Stillness again, this time of menace, isolation, lack of community. There is a clever, slightly surrealist touch (reminiscent of Russian film techniques in the Twenties) in the last line of the first verse.
Several common symbols will be recognized: e.g. mountain, waterfall. The epithets in the last line of verse 2 (and others) are worth attention.

UNDERNEATH THE ABJECT WILLOW (L.S. XXII–2. p. 54)
The second of *Two Poems for Benjamin Britten* (the composer).

FISH IN THE UNRUFFLED LAKES (L.S. XXVII. p. 60)
A common contrast in Auden: the 'innocence' of the animal kingdom compared with man, who carries the weight of consciousness in Time.
The epithets 'shadowed' and 'narrow' are interesting.

O WHO CAN EVER PRAISE ENOUGH (L.I. p. 143)
(from 'W.H.A. to E.M.A.' No. 2)
Auden says this poem was suggested by 'a picture of the Seven Ages of Man'. Again, we see his love of incantation, especially of incantatory dread.

ABLE AT TIMES TO CRY (A.T. Pt. I. No. I. p. 15)
Man, living in Time and with roots in history and family, on a spiritual journey. There are some finely evocative and symbolic touches, and the poem is as hopeful as Auden's poems usually are. There are also, as often, some looser features.

a living gun: perhaps meant to be a near pun on the name of Livingstone, a nineteenth-century missionary and explorer

LULLABY (A.T. Pt. I. No. XVIII. p. 43)
Probably the best known of Auden's love lyrics, celebrating a

moment of calm, of gentleness and peace, snatched from disorder.

ORPHEUS (A.T. Pt. I. No. XIX. p. 45)
This haunting poem is about being-and-wonder, knowledge-and-will, the urgent desire to know and the simple acceptance of life—all these as contrasts.

Orpheus: poet and musician in Greek legend

SONG (A.T. XXIX. p. 61)

NEW YEAR LETTER (lines 1651–1707. pp. 73–5)
This, the poem's final Invocation, is a lyric cry to God, in belief and humility. Here is an instance of Auden's later 'Love' = 'agape' (the love of God).

unicorn: this mythical creature could be captured only by a virgin, and so represented innocence and truth (and some-times Christ)

to call thy true love: this line is from an English carol

Dove: the Holy Ghost. A variant of a line in Chaucer

Icthus: Greek word for 'fish'; used as a symbol for Christ by the early Christians

Quando non fuerit: 'Since it has not existed, it does not exist', from Origen (c. A.D. 185–253), a Christian scholar

O da quod: 'O give what thou commandest, Lord', from St Augustine, *The Confessions*

Elizabeth: Elizabeth Mayer, to whom the poem is dedicated

solificatio: this word may have been invented by Auden. It seems to mean 'making for [peaceful?] solitude'.

Our life and death: from St Anthony

SONG FOR ST CECILIA'S DAY (C.S.P. Pt. III. No. VIII. p. 233)
The poem is another invocation, a celebration of man's state under God. The first section has a brilliantly interwoven pattern of internal and half-rhymes. The whole 'Song' celebrates the beauty and significance of music

St Cecilia: a Roman martyr of the third century, the patron of the blind and of musicians

TRINCULO'S SONG (S.M. Pt. II. The Supporting Cast. Sotto Voce. p. 28)
A moving comment on the job of the pathetic fool—who is one kind of writer and artist.

Trinculo: the jester in Shakespeare's *The Tempest*

SONG (N. p. 17)
The poem makes a comparison between the public and the private life, but turns round upon itself in the last verse—the really difficult problems are always personal.

Stendhal: French nineteenth-century novelist (a subtle student of power in public life)

THE DUET (N. p. 54)
purlieu: a track of land on the fringe of a forest

scrunty: from 'scrunt', meaning 'stunted' or 'worn out', especially of the stump of a tree

moskered: crumbled away

botts: diminutive for bottoms

gliddered: frozen over

THE WILLOW-WREN AND THE STARE (S.A. p. 41)
A splendid recent poem with a chorus, wry and humane. The interplay of moods—of gaiety and sadness—is finely controlled.

stare: starling

Section Four

TOO DEAR, TOO VAGUE (P. 1930. X. p. 54)
Included as an especially typical example, since this section

shows various forms and styles, of the early gnomic poetry. The probable influences are mentioned in earlier notes.

THE THREE COMPANIONS (Epilogue to OR. p. 112)
A pastiche, derived from 'The Cutty Wren' (No. 209 in *The Oxford Book of Light Verse*), of which the opening line is 'O where are you going, says Milder to Malder'. But this poem has a typical Audenesque moral: that the first step against frustration is not to give in to fear.

THE QUARRY (L.S. VI. p. 20)
A ballad, and in a common ballad mood.

SONG (L.S. XXIV. p. 56)
A pleasant comic song with a chorus. The six beggared cripples might, of course, represent great numbers of us—living in wish-fulfilment.

Garbo: a film actress very famous in the Thirties

Tantony pig: a St Anthony pig, the smallest pig of a litter. St Anthony was the patron saint of swineherds.

THE SPHINX (J.W. p. 19)
A sonnet, cleverly observed and executed; but rather self-consciously clever.

SIX SONNETS FROM 'IN TIME OF WAR' (pp. 260, 266, 269, 270, 277, 279)
These, like most of Auden's sonnets, owe much to the Austrian poet, R. M. Rilke (d. 1926). They are little allegorical fables, letting a factual story stand for abstract moral issues. Like Rilke's sonnets, they tend to jump unannounced into their narrative. Auden has not acquired Rilke's power, though he is able to acquire many of his manners; he tends to use certain devices too much, e.g. the dying fall at the end.

II: leaving Eden.

VIII: A compressed history of Western man during the last few hundred years, and of the effects of his inventions on his spirit.

XI: In Greek mythology, Ganymede was a beautiful Trojan youth who was taken to Mount Olympus and made immortal.

XII: On man's driving away the mystery from his life.

kobold: a gnome

XXI: sometimes called 'Exiles'.

ONE EVENING (A.T. Pt. I. No. XXVI. p. 55)

ROMAN WALL BLUES (A.T. Pt. II. No. V. p. 94)
Tungria: a region near the town now called Tontres, in Belgium. Numbers of its people served in the Imperial Roman armies, and some left inscriptions on the Roman Wall

fish: a symbol for Christ, to the early Christians

EPITAPH ON A TYRANT (A.T. Pt. II. No. VI. p. 95)
The final line mordantly alters the final line of Motley's *The Rise of the Dutch Republic* (1856). Motley said there, of William the Silent, 'and when he died the little children cried in the streets.'

THREE SONNETS FROM 'THE QUEST' GROUP (N.Y.L. pp. 164, 170, 172)
These are, like the earlier sonnets, allegorical.

II: The final inadequacy of intellectual activity in face of the mystery of man's life under God—a false Quest.

VIII: Another false Quest—this time one that denies Love.

X: Yet another false Quest—man's false ideas of the search for Truth. Not everyone need make a Journey.

unicorn: see earlier note (p. 214)

LEAP BEFORE YOU LOOK (C.S.P. 135)
Auden is enjoying using a mathematical form which seems to be of his own invention. It has six four-line verses on only two rhymes. The rhyme-scheme of each verse is different from the rest; thus the poem uses all the possible combinations of such a form.

A witty versifying of the necessity for choice—the Leap is the existentialist 'leap in the dark' into faith. Kierkegaard (*d.* 1885), the Danish Christian philosopher, is the main influence here.

A HEALTHY SPOT (C.S.P. 144)
The setting is an American campus and the figures probably American academic staff and their wives.
Relaxed, low-temperature, occasional verse, and very witty. But that 'alone' at the end is surely more smart than true?
clambakes: picnics (American)

IF I COULD TELL YOU (C.S.P. 146)
A villanelle
On Time as meaningless (but demanding) in itself; the meaning of life lies outside Time.

ALONSO TO FERDINAND (S.M. Pt. II. The Supporting Cast. Sotto Voce. p. 22)
Alonso, on board ship and bound for Naples, is saying farewell to kingship in his son's favour.
The heavily-accented verse seems to be Auden's own creation. It has an elaborate and difficult rhyme-scheme. Auden may have derived something here from the American poet, Marianne Moore. How is the half-dreamlike atmosphere created?
efreet: a demon in Mohammedan mythology
Ecbatana: ancient capital of the Medes
statue move: see Shakespeare's *The Winter's Tale*, V. 3

MIRANDA'S SONG. (S.M. Pt. II. The Supporting Cast. Sotto Voce. p. 29)
Miranda is celebrating her new-found love for Ferdinand. Her childhood terrors have gone; she is full of thankfulness and joy.
A villanelle. How does the form assist the mood, help to create the atmosphere of quiet and loving musing?

The first line has been justly called 'intricately vague'. What meaning would you give to it?

THE AGE OF ANXIETY (Pt. II. The Seven Ages. p. 34)
Quant, a dusty middle-aged clerk, is here describing his child-hood. The landscape is that industrial landscape so frequently found in Auden, a land of magical gaunt beauty. The details are well caught.

Auden is using a modification of the Anglo-Saxon verse line (see earlier note on *The Age of Anxiety*).

hammer pond: a dammed-up pond used to provide power for small local iron-works

THE RAKE'S PROGRESS (pp. 22–3.)
Included as an example of Auden's skill in writing operatic libretti (see the Introduction). Shadow, the Devil in disguise, is singing.

WALKS (H.C. p. 64)
The light, tripping tetrameters have obviously been chosen deliberately. To good purpose, do you think?

Auden muses over different kinds of walk: *purposive* walks, straight there and back to do something; and *purposeless* walks, walks for pure fun or recreation, walks inspired by 'a fidget in the soul'—walks which go in a circle to end where they began, at home. The walks become little symbols for problems of choice, decision and purpose (e.g. the circular walk turns 'behaviour into deed'; animals simply 'behave', whereas men commit 'deeds', that is, willed and ordered actions).

Section Five

THE QUESTION (P. 1930. XXVII. p. 83)
Early gnomic poem, on will and decision.

LAW LIKE LOVE (A.T. Pt. I. No. II. p. 17)
A witty poem on some of Auden's major themes. What is Law?
The different meanings given to it (Law is here what Auden
elsewhere calls Necessity). Law is, finally, like 'Love': though
here 'Love' has its later, Christian, complexity.

THE PROPHETS (A.T. Pt. I. No. IX. p. 29)
This is a transitional poem, on the moment of realizing that one
believes in God. The landscape symbol is now familiar.

The Good Place: from Henry James

adit: see earlier note (p. 203)

ANOTHER TIME (A.T. Pt. I. No. XXX. p. 62)
Living in Time; choice; freely willing—the poem plays across
these themes.

NEW YEAR 'LETTER
(a) lines 99–126, pp. 20–1
The ideas here owe much to Rilke. Auden is celebrating the
work of writers and artists.

Hunted you out of life: this is the Freudian idea of artistic creation
as compensation for inability in practical life. It occurs also in
Kierkegaard

(b) lines 860–913, pp. 47–8
On living in Time, Becoming not Being. But occasionally we
may have moments of Love and of Being; then we return to
our positive engagement in Time. A touch of the familiar
Thirties menace can be seen.

Temenos: a region of tabu, which in ancient times signified a
piece of land or a grove consecrated to the God

(c) lines 1519–1546, pp. 68–9
On Building the Just City, a civil society. In the loneliness of
mass technological societies we can see that we are all, finally,
alone. Accept this condition, Auden says, but act positively.

Here: i.e. in the U.S.A.